Jill Hellwig is more than just an author—she is a transformational leader, an inspiring friend, and a beacon of light for anyone striving to grow into their God-given potential. Her books, *Grow with Goals* and *Go with Goals,* have profoundly impacted my life by teaching me how to set meaningful goals, align them with my values, and pursue them with clarity and purpose.

Jill's unwavering commitment to Christian principles shines through in everything she does. Her wisdom and guidance have helped me not only achieve my dreams but also discover deeper truths about myself along the journey. She has a remarkable gift for helping others uncover their unique strengths and navigate life's challenges with grace and determination.

Through her mentorship and friendship, Jill has reminded me that with faith, focused effort, and a heart for growth, there are no limits to what we can achieve. I am forever grateful for her influence and her passion for helping people live their best lives.

Heather A. Prichard
Broker, Ziglar Realty
Broker, Prichard Real Estate Group

GO WITH GOALS

40 DAYS OF FOCUS TO KEEP MOVING FORWARD

JILL HELLWIG

Go with Goals
40 Days of Focus to Keep Moving Forward
Jill Hellwig

To contact the author:
jill@brandnewu.org

Send permission requests to info@brandnewu.org
Attention: Permissions Coordinator

Published by:

Mary Ethel

Mary Ethel Eckard
Frisco, Texas

Library of Congress Catalog Number: 2025904808
ISBN (Paperback): 978-1-966561-08-8
ISBN (eBook): 978-1-966561-09-5

Other Books by Jill Hellwig:
Grow With Goals, A How-To Guide for Activating Your Purpose

This book is dedicated to my dear sons,
Evan, Elijah and Ethan Hellwig,
and all of the incredibly resilient young adults in their generation.

Evan, Elijah and Ethan, I am so proud of how hard you have worked
in these last years. You are now ready to GO into all the world. You
each have an indomitable spirit and will rise to meet every challenge.
I pray you always *Go with Goals*, but even more importantly, Go
with God. He is with you and will never fail. I love you!

SPECIAL THANKS

Bob Goff says, "God doesn't give us maps to follow; He
gives us people to Go with." These are my people:

I could not have created this book without my editor
and publisher, Mary Ethel Eckard.
Mary, you have made my literary dreams come true! Thank you for your
creative genius, gentle guidance and ready words. Thank you for your
encouragement on my writing journey and for keeping me focused and
moving forward. Thank you for your partnership as we help others tell their
story too. I am truly humbled at what God can do with two willing vessels.
I love you, Mary!

Thank you to Bruce Barbour, Laurie Magers, Michelle Prince, Dana Robinson,
Lisa Williams and Aisha Willis for your expertise over the years and guiding me
at various stages in this project. Your talent, insights and wisdom are a gift!

To my Ziglar Family and my Parents—Each of my projects is a testament
to the foundation and concepts you've taught me since I was 16 years
old. I am forever grateful for your impact and influence in my life.

To my husband and my kids—all of this is for you. Thank you for
being willing to let me share our stories. I love you so much.

To my Lord and Savior Jesus Christ—All the glory goes to you forever!

Contents

Preface

A new cycle and season have begun.
The holding pattern in America (and the world) is over.
I declare: YOUR holding pattern is over.

In 2020, a cycle began that put us corporately into a stuck place in life. During that time, we endured multiple losses, setbacks, and unprecedented roadblocks. Conflict was rampant; our families, young adults and children were attacked.

Despite the opposition, some took the time to grow in this season. We dug deep, got closer to God and His word and held on. We cried tears, we moved through as best we knew how, we got help and we leaned into the lessons. We connected with new communities. Many people moved and created new alignments. We sharpened our skills, got educated, burned the midnight oil and did what needed to be done to make up for the lack.

For those who did that, a new day is dawning. The seeds you planted were watered with your sweat and tears. You forged a new trail and became a pioneer for the next era. Let me affirm you.

Some, instead of growing, fell asleep and stayed on the sidelines during this time. We couldn't take the pain, so we dug a hole and went into our caves. Lured by comfort, media and fear. Addictions set in, burdens were compounded and now we're not sure what to do.

If this is you, it is okay!! You are not behind. Get up now and go back to what your fathers taught you. Eradicate fear, hang ups, toxic situations and people from your life. A fresh grace is upon you if you receive it. You can go where you want to go, and you have the opportunity to do what you want to do. The choice is yours.

Most of us are probably somewhere in between these two extremes. We've grown, and yet maybe we've stayed on the sidelines too long.

This book is for any of us, at any level.

> A new day has dawned.
> It's Show Time.
> It's Go Time!
> It's Game Time!!

As you dive into this book, I have a few ideas for you. First, read Jeremiah 33:3 and ask, "God, what do you want to show me?"

Next, read Matthew 18:19 and ask, "God, where and to whom do you want me to GO?"

Finally, read Acts 2:40-42 and strengthen your team. Ask, "God, to whom am I called and where should I belong?"

> Your holding pattern is over.
> It's a brand new day!

Please remember this: the book's tagline is 40 Days of Focus to Keep Moving Forward. This book is going to help you more than ever before to keep moving toward your goals.

This book is a sequel to *Grow with Goals*. In that book, you learned all about yourself and what's most important to you in life. By the end of the book, you set four priority goals.

Go with Goals is now the tool you need to stay focused while implementing those four priority goals.

In just a few minutes, you are going to turn the next page, and we are going to dive in deep quickly.

The next pages are a treasure trove of information that I have lived out and practiced regularly for over two decades. The process works. That's one of the reasons I appreciate your taking the time to read this work, because I want it to work for you so badly.

You've done the hard work of setting your goals the right way.
Now, it's **Go Time** for you.

Don't get weary as you go through these 40 days. If that pace is too quick for you, finish it in 40 weeks. You are not in a contest that you have to win. Take this material at your own pace and finish strong in your own time. I believe your life will be forever changed.

Cheering you on!
Let's Go!

Foreword

Have you ever been in the company of someone who was an expert at *something*, and then you got to know them and found out they have been doing that *something* for most of their years on planet earth? This is my wife, Jill, and she is an expert on goal setting and achieving.

When we were dating, I would go to her house, and she would have goals written on paper using a pen, pencil, marker or crayon. She was serious about setting and reaching her goals. During our 27 years of marriage, she has been consistent with this behavior.

After we were married, her parents brought us the treasure chest from their attic that contained her childhood things. As we went through it, there were her Houston Oilers pom poms, stuffed animals, and journals. We opened a journal from her 6th grade year and began to read. Guess what? The journal was filled with her short-term and long-term goals like the college she wanted to attend and the grade she wanted to make in math. I was amazed at the discipline of a young middle school kid who wrote out their goals of what they wanted in life. I mean, I just wanted to win the tetherball match at recess.

As you start applying the principles of this book, please know they have been tested and proven in her life over and over and over. You can trust your deepest desires and dreams to this process because I've watched ours come to fruition in our marriage.

One of Jill's deepest desires is to see others reach their goals. She cares about people becoming all they were born to be. You may have never written a goal, or you may be a goal setter; either way, this book will help you get from where you are to where you want to be! When you put your trust in this process, you can put in the work that it takes to meet the goals.

A set goal can only be accomplished by daily working to achieve it. I know because I watched Jill achieve her goals by setting them and then working daily to achieve what she wrote. The life of goals set and met is a journey and you have picked an amazing person to partner with since I know she has the determination to see it through. Thank you for trusting her to help you be all you can be!

Tell us about your journey anytime! We love hearing the testimony of the process.

Jill's husband,
Jay Hellwig

Introduction

Hello Go Getter!

Today is going to be a great day. You have everything within you to make it so, but it can be difficult to stay on track, reduce distractions, and balance all of life's responsibilities. With so many pressures and commitments, it's common to tackle the things that scream the loudest first, meaning you never quite make it to what matters most. You know the saying— "the squeaky wheel gets the grease." In the middle of noisy distractions, there are steps you can take to ground yourself for growth and forward motion. This book has the answers and practical steps to finding focus, maintaining priorities, getting ahead of life's ever-present demands and being proactive rather than reactive. You'll learn to oil all the wheels, giving them just the right amount of attention, reducing the loudest squeaks, while still getting what you need.

But how? Finding perspective and maintaining balance requires encouragement, effort, accountability and understanding. This requires you to stop instinctively reacting to the noises, instead focusing your time and attention on understanding the core areas of your life. Where are your strengths and weaknesses? Where do you thrive and where do you need improvement? How can you shift your focus from reactive emergencies to proactive living? There are answers to pull you out of the chaos, but each comes with preparation and evaluation of the areas where the balance is off in your life. I believe this is not an elusive goal. You can have the life you've always wanted, successful across the board, in all the realms that matter most. Not only will we push forward on meeting your four priority goals for your work or family, but we will also focus on your personal goals, helping you identify areas in your life that may be off balance.

I am a trained professional carrying forth the legacy of the great Zig Ziglar. Years ago, he adopted what he called "The Wheel of Life." It is comprised of seven spokes, each representing a core area of our lives. The spokes are: Spiritual, Physical, Mental, Personal, Family, Financial, and Career. When each spoke of the wheel is balanced, life runs smoother, giving you space and time to plan ahead rather than reacting to imbalances. When you take the time to develop each spoke, your wheel gets stronger and spins evenly. You grow, your life runs smoother and faster, and you have the necessary momentum to propel you forward.

During this 40-day transformational journey, you will review each of these areas to assess your strengths and weaknesses. You will focus on one core area (wheel spoke) per week. Your daily devotions include action items to strengthen your weaknesses and celebrate your strengths. If you put in the effort, you will learn to have holistic balance in every aspect of your life. Though it sounds daunting, it doesn't have to be. Take it day by day, one step at a time. A radically different life will soon open up before you, and you will realize how far you have come.

Let's look at The Wheel of Life to see what you can learn about yourself. Where are you now on the journey to achieving your limitless potential?

THE WHEEL OF LIFE

(Created by Zig Ziglar)

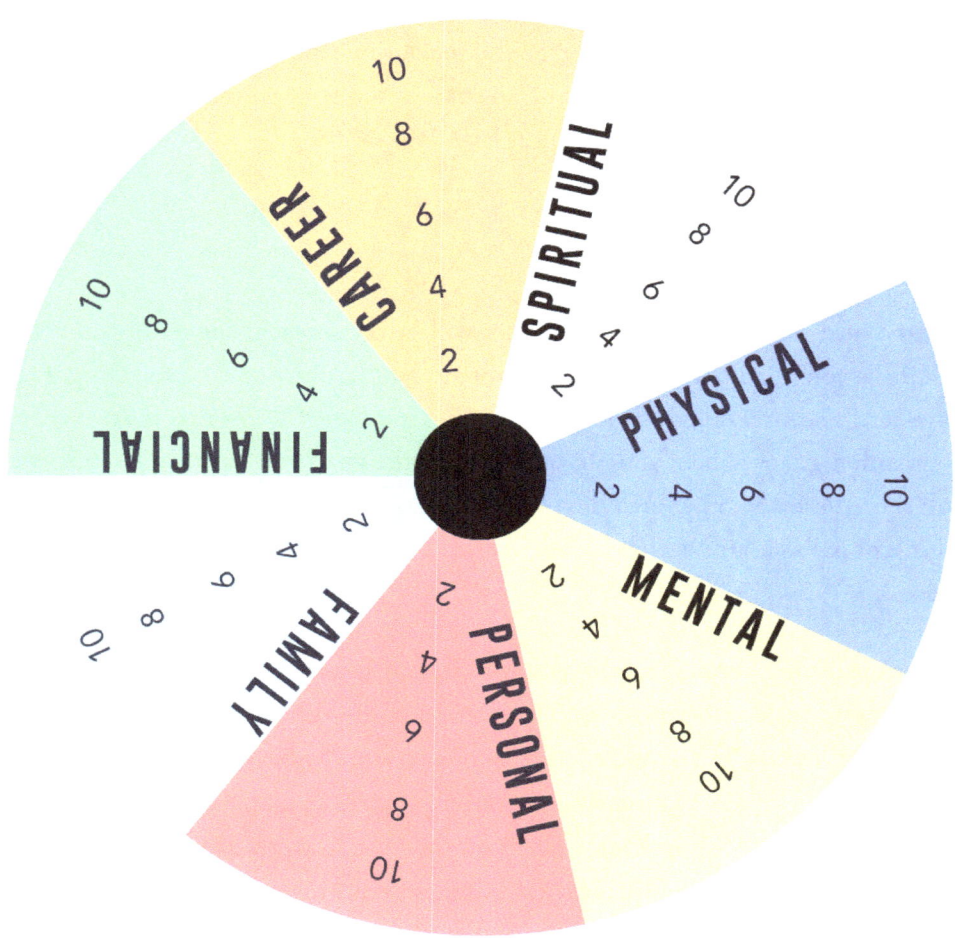

Seven core areas of life are shown on the wheel above with a scale of numbers below the name of each. Take a moment to meditate on your life and evaluate your personal health in each area. Then, when you are ready, grab a pen or pencil to rate yourself on a scale of 1-10 by circling the appropriate number in each spoke.

After finishing all seven spokes, draw a line connecting the circled number within the wheel.

To possess true fulfillment, you want to have a measure of success in each spoke of the wheel. How bumpy would your ride be if you used this current version of your wheel to try to get you somewhere?

Throughout your life, there are moments when you will be out of balance; that is okay. The goal is to give yourself grace and to continue moving forward with a focus on improving in all areas. The goal is to smooth out your wheel over your lifetime so that every area of your life can be at level 10 quality.

THE NEXT 40 DAYS

For the next 40 days, our focus together will be on different spokes of the Wheel of Life as you pursue fulfillment and contentment in every area of your life. If you have read and/or worked through my book, *Grow with Goals,* this is an excellent companion guide to help you not only achieve the goals you have set, but also help you shore up every other area of your life, creating a whole you, a brand new you. Think of me as your coach, guiding you on this journey, cheering you on toward success.

At the beginning of each section, you will find an 11-question quiz to help you rate yourself on a scale of 1-5 regarding that section in the Wheel of Life. The best score you can achieve is 55 (11 questions all scored a number 5). For those items where your score is 5, that's a cause for celebration. For those items where your score is between 1 and 3, consider listing them on the journal pages as potential areas for growth. Then journal a few ideas focusing on ways to improve your lifestyle in those areas.

I remember this old adage used by my grandparents, "55 saves lives." This was a slogan in the 1970s for going 55 mph on the highway. In the case of your Wheel of Life, 55 will not only save your life, but it will increase your level of fulfillment and satisfaction immensely. You might not be anywhere near 55 today, and that's okay. It simply means you have an opportunity for growth.

It is interesting to me that the biblical meaning for the number 5 is grace. Grace gives us empowerment and covering. It is a gift we cannot earn ourselves. As you go through this process, focus on that score of 55. I believe you have double grace for this process in this time and season. Give yourself all the grace you can and receive it from and give it to others as you stay focused on this journey. Keep moving forward with graceful living in mind.

SETTING DAILY GOALS TO ACHIEVE BALANCE

As you work through each daily devotion, pay specific attention to the daily action items. You may feel compelled to set goals to strengthen this core area of your life. The following system was developed to help me with my daily goal setting and prioritizing my to-do list. It will also be helpful for you to keep your mind focused and grease your own wheels to keep them running smoothly and quietly.

Practicing the skills outlined in this book has been vital for me with all the demands of daily life. I've used this process throughout my personal life and career to stay on track and complete many successful ventures. From being a top sales professional in corporate America full-time, to going part-time, to full-time ministry and community service and to now owning my own business, this process helped me navigate with clarity. I've used it at home as well, in our 27 year marriage, raising four children (our oldest is twenty-two and our youngest is ten), taking care of our home and finances, moving through many seasons and decades of life. Many well-meaning people have been confused by my unusual methods, because I don't have a "fake it til you make it," "hustle and grind" mentality, but I have seen incredible success. The process within these pages will work for you if you are a corporate executive, entrepreneur, stay-at-home parent, have a full-time job, or are a student.

Discernment, prayer and clarity helped me stay on track and focused. Instead of setting a rigid to-do list for each day, I came up with a 3-part system for success to increase my joy, efficiency and effectiveness, so I could literally "go" for the goals and big dreams I've had, while also staying faithful to my daily responsibilities.

MY 3 PART
PRODUCTIVITY SYSTEM

We will put my 3 Part Productivity System to use at the beginning of each week throughout this 40 day journey. Let's Go!

PART 1
THE MOST IMPORTANT
MEETING OF THE WEEK

At the beginning of every week that I worked at the Ziglar Corporation, staff and guests would start the week with devotions. This was a 30-minute meeting set aside for an inspirational speaker to encourage us to start our week with God. Mr. Ziglar called this meeting, "the most important meeting we will hold in our company this week."

If you are like most people, you hate meetings. Taking the time out of your busy day to focus on someone else's priorities on their schedule is a drain, to say the least. But this meeting isn't like that one. The most important meeting of your week is your weekly *POWER Meeting*. Instead of thinking about it as a meeting, think of it as your weekly huddle to discuss strategies, making sure everyone is on the same page. Or consider it like a pep rally, where everyone comes together to do their part to move the team forward toward everyone's goals.

You can apply this formula whether you're a team of 1, 4 or 40. You can apply it to a meeting between yourself and God first, a meeting with your family second, and a meeting with your work and/or social teams next. This time together is invaluable and necessary for the entire system to work efficiently.

While it is different for everyone, and circumstances change from week to week, there are a few necessary components to a successful weekly *POWER Meeting*:

- Bring your calendar.
- Bring your current goals and needs for the coming week.
- Commit your week to God and each other.

Each meeting will take a different form. Some are in the conference room with a whiteboard, some around the kitchen table and some are standing meetings, only lasting 5-7 minutes. If it's a family *POWER Meeting*, sometimes the meetings are during Sunday dinner or even the halftime of Sunday Night Football. If it's a work *POWER meeting*, perhaps we gather every Thursday at lunch or Wednesday every other week at 1:00 over Zoom.

Sometimes these check-ins are brief moments in your family room, the hallway outside your offices, the car on the way to an event. The meetings aren't always perfect, but the point is to connect. Connect with your thoughts with your calendar, and with each other.

You will be amazed as your goals stay on track, at your entire team's focus, and how you keep progressing when you are in agreement with the teams that matter most in your life.

These agreements allow you to move forward in your personal responsibilities with clarity and peace.

In Matthew 18:19-20, Jesus taught His disciples about the exponential power that exists when we are in agreement with each other. He said, *"Again, I say to you, that if two of you shall agree on the earth as touching anything that they shall ask, it shall be done for them of my Father, which is in heaven. For where two or three are gathered together in my name, there am I in the midst of them."*

Author, teacher and founder of Christian Men's Network, Edwin Louis Cole, said it like this, "Communication is the basis of life. Exchange is the process of life. Agreement is the power of life."

When you are intentional, your weekly *POWER Meeting* creates synergy within your group. Whether it is just you and your Creator, you

> "The place of agreement is the place of power."
> Matthew 18:19

and your family, you and your work team, you and your coach, or you and your friends, this promised principle frames your focus and effectiveness going forward.

I have seen this principle work in my own life. And I've also seen my goals waiver when I don't actively pursue agreement. It's quite easy for disagreement to come in and cause confusion, goal diffusion, discouragement and drift. Reaching goals and staying focused is hard enough without all of the distractions. Your most important meeting of the week is your *POWER Meeting*.

To find a place of agreement, I recommend implementing the agenda for your meeting using an acronym for the word *POWER*, as explained on the next page. (I suggest you earmark that page so you can easily refer back to it.) When we agree together as companies, friends, ministries, families, there is power in our agreement and our results are dynamic. (Note: *POWER Meetings* can be held among family members, co-workers, friends, committees, organizations, etc.)

At the beginning of each chapter, you will be provided a *POWER* form to complete in response to the decisions made in your meeting. Remember this is a significant step in achieving your goals.

THE MOST IMPORTANT MEETING OF THE WEEK

P

PRAYER REQUEST

We start and end each meeting in prayer, and we seek, depending on time, to take requests individually. We then make sure someone on the team is praying for each person, as well as for the meeting we are about to have. We pray for synergy, unity, ideas, inspiration and agreement. We invite God's presence into our situation.

O

OLD BUSINESS

This is a time to review what was accomplished in the past week:
- What did we check off our lists? We celebrate these goals achieved.
- What is still pending and what activities need to be continued this week?

Each team member gives an update to the projects they owned.
We add updates and follow up "to-do" items in our notes and calendars

W

WHAT'S NEXT?

What "new business" is coming up this week?
- Are there any specific events for one member of the team we all need to attend?
- Are there any big projects where we each need to contribute?

This can be a time for ideation and brainstorming. Perhaps one of the more visionary team members shares a futuristic thought or picture. Take new ideas and sift through them with the following expectations and roles in mind.

E

EXPECTATIONS

- What expectations do we have for ourselves in the coming week?
- What expectations do we have of others?
- What people, deadlines, celebrations, and milestones are coming up?
- Who do we want to bless this week?
- What is coming up in the lives of others, and how can we be tuned in to their needs?

Here we define how we will measure success for a particular project.

R

ROLES, RESPONSIBILITIES, AND RESOURCES

- What tasks and chores are needed to be fulfilled by each team member to accomplish our goals this week?
- What homework, work goals, and responsibilities are the priority?
- Who has what responsibilities?
- Who owns which tasks?
- Who is accountable to the work at hand?
- What resources are needed to accomplish our goals?

"The place of agreement is the place of power." Matthew 18:19

PART 2

NIGHTLY BRAIN RELEASE

"Your future depends on your dreams, so go to sleep!"

-M. BARAZANI

We are busy people and often sacrifice our time of rest and sleep to be more productive or *get just one more thing* done. Sometimes we are exhausted and ready to sleep, but we can't because of all the events of the day, the worries of tomorrow, and potential issues in the future swirling around in our brains. Does this sound familiar at all? I know this cycle all too well.

I found the best way for this productivity system to work is to do a nightly brain release. You can't wake up in the morning, empty and ready to listen, if your mind is still full from the day before.

More than a decade ago, I began using a checklist each night before bed. I now use a specific journal where I write prayers to God about my day and things that concern me. I write everything that comes to my mind: responsibilities, emotions, expectations and thoughts that need to be excavated so they can be organized. I ask God to give me His perspective on the items and I jot down what I believe He said to me. I write about this in *Grow with Goals* on pages 26 & 27. Perhaps journaling or writing things in your calendar before bedtime will help. Regardless of what you do, the goal is to get all the thoughts that concern you out of your head to experience restful sleep. You can also conclude your workday with a brain release similar to this.

I believe we experience power in this process because we surrender and cast our cares on Him. Each time I write out my list or prayer to God, trusting Him to take care of it, I submit to Him. I release the burden to Him. I'm not just dumping this information somewhere to someone who doesn't care. I am releasing it to a loving Creator Who knows me from the inside out, has a perspective much higher than mine and Whom I trust to partner with me to take care of the concerns of my heart.

When you release the day's activities, your concerns, your hopes and dreams to a Higher Power, you admit you can't control it all and actively decide to submit to Someone Who can. You receive love as a child of God and rest, knowing that He knows how to care for you and yours better than you do. You are once again giving your goals back to God.

Consider using the following checklist and then develop a system that works best for you:

NIGHTLY CHECKLIST TO CLEAR YOUR MIND

☐ Pause	☐ Take out contacts	☐ Contemplate life
☐ Reflect on the day	☐ Take a bath	☐ Ponder deeply
☐ Clean up	☐ Stretch	☐ Think positively
☐ Pack lunches	☐ Change into PJs	☐ Reject insomnia
☐ Empty trash	☐ Brush teeth	☐ Meditate
☐ Check email	☐ Floss	☐ Pray
☐ Check thermostat	☐ Wash face	☐ Use bathroom again
☐ Charge cell phone	☐ Say good nights	☐ Get a glass of water
☐ Lock door	☐ Read	☐ Adjust pillows
☐ Set alarm	☐ Relax	☐ Count blessings
☐ Turn out the lights	☐ Scroll/Watch television	☐ Count sheep
☐ Check weather	☐ Play peaceful music	☐ Journal
☐ Pick out outfit	☐ Turn off television	☐ Surrender
☐ Use bathroom	☐ Breathe deeply	☐ Release Control

NIGHTLY BRAIN RELEASE - JOURNALING

My thoughts, ideas, concerns and worries

- [ ] Family dentist appointments
- [ ] Discuss with mom retirement account plans
- [ ] Declutter pantry before grocery shopping this week
- [ ] This week's soccer schedule - I need to clone myself!
- [ ] Complete year-end report on time!
- [ ] Create year-end report presentation (think positive!)
- [ ]
- [ ]
- [ ]
- [ ]

What is God saying about these items?

- [ ] Psalm 37:5: "Commit your way to the Lord. Trust also in Him. and He will do it."
- [ ]
- [ ]
- [ ]
- [ ]
- [ ]

Now that we've laid the groundwork and you've set up your *POWER Meeting* and have your brain release in order, you can sleep peacefully. When you wake up, you will be ready for part 3.

FOLLOWING THE SIGNALS TO SUCCESS - GREEN, YELLOW, RED LIGHT SYSTEM

As my responsibilities in life expanded, I needed a better way to prioritize my goals. Each morning, I made time to pray, read scripture and get in touch with my spirit. I came into agreement first with what God wanted me to do for the day. I still use this practice daily and it keeps my mind focused on the things that matter most. I often review my nightly brain release or journal notes to determine what needs to be dealt with immediately and what I can reprioritize to the bottom of the list.

Then, I meditate on these items and pray, asking for a picture in my mind, just like the signal at a stoplight. I imagine myself waiting at a red stoplight. I envision myself in all of that traffic, just sitting there, asking God to show me when the light turns green and then if it turns yellow and then red again. I ask for confirmation through scripture or sometimes through encouragement or the words of other people, and then I assign each task, thought or project with a green light, yellow light, or red light.

Then, I add green light items to my daily calendar, sometimes as meetings in my phone or simply writing them on my productivity schedule (provided at the beginning of each chapter). I make a note of yellow and red light items on a master list in my journal or under the green light items. This exercise helps me maintain focus, patience, and meet demands on time.

The ability to do this well doesn't happen immediately but comes over time with consistent use and accountability. Trust yourself, trust your instincts and give yourself grace when things don't go quite right. You will get there!

GREEN LIGHT (G)

Go! Time to move.

If you feel a particular item is a green light, pursue it with all your energy. Act quickly and don't hesitate. That green means "strike while the iron is hot."

Even if you aren't at work, if you sense a green light to call a client, even while running an errand or taking a child to the park, stop and contact the client when you have a quiet moment.

As I began to use this process, my timing with people improved. Time after time, they would answer or text back, "I'm so glad you reached out; I was just thinking I needed to contact you today."

Developing impeccable timing is one of your most valuable keys to seeing success. You must be able to discern when it is time to move and when it is time to stay.

YELLOW LIGHT (Y)

Yield. Not a priority.

If an item is a yellow light, it is not the most important thing and can be moved lower down on your list. After you've completed all of your green light items, you can feel free to complete these yellow light items if you have time.

Yellow can mean yielding to another person or another season. Maybe this particular item is an opportunity to collaborate with someone or take a look at the item from a different angle.

Often, I find when I sense a yellow light, that I can choose what to do. I can go or I can wait. It isn't a priority, so I just keep it in the back of my mind, stay open and watchful, looking for signs and signals to bring it to the front.

RED LIGHT (R)

Pause. Wait. Search for clarity.

As you are praying about your week ahead and day ahead, a particular project you talked about in your *POWER meeting,* conversation or relationship and you sense a red light, consider pushing it out one week.

There were times when I felt a red light in my sales career, meaning not to call a particular client or prospect that day, but, at the behest of some persistent co-workers, I pursued that lead anyway. Those efforts proved unsuccessful, and I found it was much more productive to pursue those green items, letting the red items percolate.

You must be able to discern when it is time to move and when it is time to wait. A red light will require discipline and trust in God to tell you when to move.

PRODUCTIVITY SCHEDULE

WEEK OF:

SUNDAY

G Y R
G Y R
G Y R
G Y R

MONDAY

G Y R
G Y R
G Y R
G Y R

TUESDAY

G Y R
G Y R
G Y R
G Y R

WEDNESDAY

G Y R
G Y R
G Y R
G Y R

THURSDAY

G Y R
G Y R
G Y R
G Y R

FRIDAY

G Y R
G Y R
G Y R
G Y R

SATURDAY

G Y R
G Y R
G Y R
G Y R

MY TOP 4 PRIORITY GOALS

○ _____
○ _____
○ _____
○ _____

THIS WEEK'S TOP THREE PRIORITIES, PROJECTS & PEOPLE

○ _____
○ _____
○ _____

IMPORTANT NOTES

Using this 3 Part Productivity System gives you clarity, peace of mind and integrity in your actions and interactions. You will respond to the demands of daily life with your personal goals and your team in mind and you will surrender your progress and output to a God who has impeccable timing. After all, He hung the stars, moon, sun and planets. I think we can trust Him to plan our lives as well.

Using this system does make life more unpredictable. Practically speaking, it means you don't always set a day on your calendar when you just know you are going to call a person back to make progress on a project. It means you put the date on your calendar and follow the initiatives from your *POWER Meeting* and your journal about it at night or in the morning. When that day arrives, pray and ask God to tell you if it is the right time to follow up.

It means even if it isn't on your calendar, and even if it seems you don't have time to do it that day, but you sense a green light, you make contacting that person or advancing that project a priority.

If it is on your calendar and you sense a red light, you wait until you sense you have a yellow or green. This type of movement requires great patience, stamina and reliance on the Holy Spirit. Follow the signals to success. If you approach each decision with the mindset of a focused Go Getter, you will enjoy this process. You will come to realize how wonderful it is to trust in God and others to help you reach your goals, not on your own efforts or back-breaking hard work. Yes, you will be working, but you won't be a slave to your goals. You won't lose your health or your relationships in the process of achievement. You rely on the wind of the Holy Spirit to carry you forward as you do ALL He has created you to do since the beginning of time. You WILL move forward.

You can do this! I believe in you!

Now that we have established my 3 Part Productivity System, we are ready to go. Let us not become stagnant in our growth. When we take time to understand our strengths and weaknesses in each spoke of the wheel, when we have discovered our special gifts and talents, then we can meld these areas together and learn to achieve and succeed. In my book, *Grow with Goals*, we also worked through discovering our truest inner desires, core values, and purpose in life, which play a great role in setting goals that work with us rather than against us. Keep these core values, desires, and purpose in mind as you work through this devotional to assess and improve the core areas of your life.

Go with Goals is a companion guide to the *Grow with Goals* workbook, but it can also be used as a standalone devotion. My initial plan was to include devotions throughout *Grow with Goals* to keep people motivated. As it turned out, the devotions seemed to get lost when combined with the other information. But as an encourager, I couldn't let goal achievers work toward goals without extra focus, inspiration and action items.

If you know the goals you have, both long-term and short-term, include them on the following page, as a reminder of what you are working toward. I found working on just four goals at a time helps me stay focused and remain efficient. If you need help developing your goals and steps, read my book, *Grow with Goals*. You can work through both of these books at the same time or separately. Now, you are ready to begin with your Top 4 Priority Goals and 3 Part Productivity System to stay on track.

Let's go!

HELLWIG

NEXT 90 DAYS - TOP FOUR GOALS

If you know the goals you have, both long-term and short-term, include them on the following page, as a reminder of what you are working toward. I found working on just four goals at a time helps you stay focused and remain efficient. If you need help developing your goals and steps, read my book, Grow with Goals. You can work through both of these books at the same time or separately. Now, you are ready to begin with your Top 4 Priority Goals and 3 Part Productivity System to stay on track.

In Grow with Goals, you identified the top four goals you want to achieve and are willing to work toward. To keep you on track, list those four goals below, in the space provided.

GOAL 1

GOAL 2

GOAL 3

GOAL 4

When you are losing focus or motivation, come back to this list and remember what you are working toward. You can do this!

How to Use this Book

WEEKLY POWER MEETING, BRAIN RELEASE AND GREEN/YELLOW/RED LIGHT SYSTEM

At the beginning of each chapter, you will find forms to create your 3 Part Productivity Schedule for the week. This form can be completed after the most important meeting of the week, your *POWER Meeting*. A sample form is shown at the end of this chapter, which includes the green light items, breaking them into the five days of the week, where they best seem to fit. After you have completed the green light items, list the yellow light and red light items. Be sure to check the items off as they are completed, and do not stress if everything doesn't get done. Family emergencies, outings, and distractions will always exist. Simply give yourself grace and work that item into the next week's productivity schedule.

Now that the productivity schedule has been completed for the week, you can focus on the self-care you need to continue making and meeting goals.

THE WHEEL OF LIFE ASSESSMENT

In this book, each new week focuses on one core spoke on the Wheel of Life. Take your time and consider each question. Circle the answer that best reflects your current lifestyle.

Based on your score, are there areas you would like to see increase in importance? Pick the areas and habits you would like to work on this week as micro goals and highlight them. What can you implement daily to increase this area of balance in your life?

DAILY ACTION ITEMS

As you move through each week, consider the action items and how they relate to the areas of improvement (micro goals) you have highlighted in that week's Wheel of Life. Be sure to journal and conduct your nightly brain release for the action items you have chosen and include your thoughts, fears, progress, etc.

Each day has a list of action items you may want to consider adding to your schedule. Take these seriously and remember to analyze, activate, and accelerate. What does this mean?

Analyze

Reflect deeply and utilize prayer each day to ground yourself as you notice recurrent patterns, thoughts, and belief systems. Listen for the still, small voice to guide you as you follow His signals for the next steps.

Activate

Don't just think about these concepts but try to put one small thing into action each day. You may have the best intentions, but resetting daily habits and actions is where true transformation is seen.

Accelerate

Remember, you are not in this alone. Utilize the resources and strengths of friends, mentors, and partners to help you arrive at your goals more efficiently and with better quality.

Use the journal pages to record your thoughts, goals, concerns, prayers, or fears. Each day, you are given an opportunity to journal your thoughts and progress toward setting and achieving your goals and action items.

THE ACTIVATOR

When I first met Jill, I couldn't have imagined the profound impact she would have on my life. At that time, I was a young adult brimming with ideas, passion, and dreams but lacking the knowledge and roadmap needed to turn those aspirations into reality. Jill is an Activator, a title that perfectly encapsulates her ability to ignite change and inspire action.

In my early years, I had an abundance of energy and ambition. I talked endlessly about the grand things I wanted to achieve, often convincing others to join me in my enthusiastic plans. However, despite my passion, that's usually where things fizzled out. My goals seemed just out of reach, and my dreams remained lofty and unattainable.

Jill changed everything. She introduced me to a comprehensive approach to goal setting that was unlike anything I had encountered before. Instead of merely aiming for the stars, Jill taught me to start by assessing my current state in all areas of my life. We identified my strengths and weaknesses and devised exercises to sharpen what was needed and replace what was useless, creating a balanced and incremental path to success. This process was transformative.

Under Jill's guidance, I learned to set realistic, achievable goals that aligned with who I was and who I aspired to become. Jill's methodology didn't just focus on the end goal but emphasized the importance of self-awareness and personal growth. She taught me that understanding myself was the key to unlocking my potential and achieving my dreams.

However, the journey was not without its hardships. There were times when circumstances seemed bleak and overwhelming, testing my resolve and determination. It wasn't always easy, and there were moments of doubt and frustration. Yet, it was in these challenging times that Jill's process truly shone. She reminded me to trust the process, to focus on incremental progress, and to keep faith in myself and the journey.

Years later, I found myself in a season of change and uncertainty. Faced with numerous life-altering decisions, I knew exactly who to call. In a difficult season of my life, when all seemed upside down, Jill provided everything I needed to discover who I was and who God made me to be. I had core values, boundaries, plans and a roadmap to be able to address future things before they even came to me. Again, Jill's approach, rooted in self-discovery and incremental progress, provided the clarity and direction I needed.

One of the most valuable lessons Jill imparted was how to align my goals with His purpose for me. This alignment not only gave me a clear sense of purpose but also helped me discern which opportunities to embrace and which to decline. By understanding who I am and what truly matters to me, I could make decisions confidently, knowing they were in harmony with my authentic self.

Working with Jill has been a journey of continuous learning and growth. Her ability to activate change is unparalleled, and her insights have been invaluable in helping me navigate life's complexities. Through her guidance, I have achieved goals I once thought impossible and discovered a deeper understanding of myself.

Jill's impact on my life is immeasurable. She has not only been a mentor and guide but also a catalyst for transformation. Her unique ability to activate change has empowered me to pursue my dreams with confidence and purpose, and for that, I am eternally grateful. This is the story of how Jill, the Activator, transformed my life and helped me become the person I am today.

Che'ree Vasquez

WEEK ONE
Spiritual Wholeness

GETTING INTO THE MINDSET OF LISTENING TO YOUR SPIRIT

The first assignment for this week is to hold the most important meeting of the week: your *POWER meeting,* so you can determine the priorities and scheduling for the week. While it is different for everyone, and circumstances change from week to week, there are a few components to the weekly meeting that are necessary for success.

- Bring your calendar.
- Bring your current goals and needs for the coming week.
- Commit your week to each other and to God.

THE MOST IMPORTANT MEETING OF THE WEEK

WEEK OF ....

P PRAYER REQUEST

O OLD BUSINESS

W WHAT'S NEXT?

E EXPECTATIONS

R ROLES, RESPONSIBILITIES, AND RESOURCES

"The place of agreement is the place of power." Matthew 18:19

NIGHTLY BRAIN RELEASE - JOURNALING

My thoughts, ideas, concerns and worries

- ☐ ....
- ☐ ....
- ☐ ....
- ☐ ....
- ☐ ....
- ☐ ....
- ☐ ....
- ☐ ....
- ☐ ....
- ☐ ....

What is God saying about these items?

- ☐ ....
- ☐ ....
- ☐ ....
- ☐ ....
- ☐ ....
- ☐ ....

PRODUCTIVITY SCHEDULE

WEEK OF:

SUNDAY

_____ G Y R

_____ G Y R

_____ G Y R

_____ G Y R

MONDAY

_____ G Y R

_____ G Y R

_____ G Y R

_____ G Y R

TUESDAY

_____ G Y R

_____ G Y R

_____ G Y R

_____ G Y R

WEDNESDAY

_____ G Y R

_____ G Y R

_____ G Y R

_____ G Y R

THURSDAY

_____ G Y R

_____ G Y R

_____ G Y R

_____ G Y R

FRIDAY

_____ G Y R

_____ G Y R

_____ G Y R

_____ G Y R

SATURDAY

_____ G Y R

_____ G Y R

_____ G Y R

_____ G Y R

MY TOP 4 PRIORITY GOALS

○ _____

○ _____

○ _____

○ _____

THIS WEEK'S TOP THREE PRIORITIES, PROJECTS & PEOPLE

○ _____

○ _____

○ _____

IMPORTANT NOTES

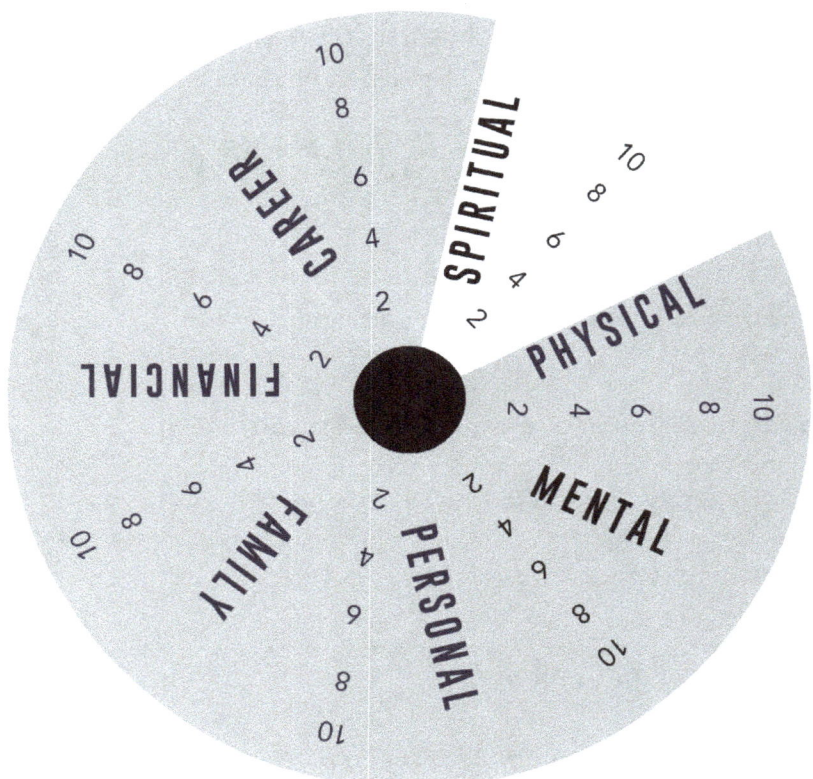

This week we will focus on our spiritual development and ensuring our foundations are in the right place. We start the journey on the spiritual spoke on the Wheel of Life. The goal of week one is to get you into the mindset of daily listening to your spirit. We will take a soft splash into the waters of change to prepare you for the deep dive that comes later in this journey.

Are you ready?

On the next page is an assessment of the Spiritual Spoke on the Wheel of Life. Take your time and consider each question. Circle the answer that best reflects your current lifestyle.

Wheel of Life

SPIRITUAL ASSESSMENT

Circle the answer that best reflects your current lifestyle.
Take the time to reflect on these.

	YOUR CURRENT LIFESTYLE	YOUR SCORE
1.	Do you believe in God?	1 2 3 4 5
2.	Do you have a sense of purpose and inner peace?	1 2 3 4 5
3.	Do you trust God and rest in His care for you?	1 2 3 4 5
4.	Do you share your faith journey with others?	1 2 3 4 5
5.	Do you meet together regularly with other believers?	1 2 3 4 5
6.	Are you a disciple of Christ?	1 2 3 4 5
7.	Are you walking out the fruit of the Spirit (love, joy, peace, patience, kindness, gentleness, goodness, faithfulness and self- control)?	1 2 3 4 5
8.	How's your prayer life?	1 2 3 4 5
9.	Do you frequently study the Bible?	1 2 3 4 5
10.	What's your level of gratitude?	1 2 3 4 5
11.	Do you have contentment and joy?	1 2 3 4 5

Total: _____

Based on your score, what are the top four lifestyle changes you would like to work on this week? List those below.

This Week's Goals

FOR LIFESTYLE CHANGE IN
THE SPIRITUAL SPOKE

GOAL 1	
GOAL 2	
GOAL 3	
GOAL 4	

What can you implement daily to increase this area of balance in your life? As you move through the week, consider the daily action items and how they relate to the four priority goals of improvement you have listed above. On the journal page, be sure to include the action items you have chosen and include your thoughts, fears, progress, etc.

It's Time to Hope

"*When there is hope for the future, there is power in the present.*"

–JOHN MAXWELL

Let's begin.

I hope you woke up with anticipation and a smile, knowing you are on the right path, headed toward good things in your future. I hope these pages assure you that your future is secure, stable, successful, and significant. You have permission and are empowered to make the changes you want to see in order to make your life more fulfilling, free, and satisfying.

Scripture says in Proverbs 13:12 NLT, "*Hope deferred makes the heart sick, but a dream fulfilled is a tree of life.*" To begin this transformation journey, it is going to take hope. It is going to take us looking through the lens of the tree of life instead of our own knowledge of good and evil.

Sometimes it's hard to hope when you've been disappointed time and time again. I find that a lot of my clients and contacts don't set goals or stop reaching for their goals because it's been too long waiting to see some things come to fruition. That is why, right at the beginning of this journey, we are going to release our dreams and goals back to God and believe that His plan is best. We are going to start fresh once again, surrender and confess to Him that we are not God and that He is, and begin with a clean slate. We are believers. From this day forward, make a commitment to rest in His loving, complete and total care for you today and every day for the rest of your time on earth.

IDEAS FOR ACTION:

- Try to find some time today to let your mind rest.

- Engage in reflection, thinking over how you're on your way to where you want to be.

- Worship today. Give thanks for all you have been given and the ability to take part in a divine plan. Humble yourself to a higher power and surrender to God's best plan.

- Spend time with those you love.

- This evening, set aside 30 minutes to one hour to take a detailed look at your planning system.

- Write this week's action steps, daily to-do lists, and end goals.

- Prepare your mind to take the necessary steps to accomplish your goals.

- Engage a friend in this journey. Contact them and ask if they will serve as your accountability and encouragement partner for the next 40 days.

JOURNAL

Based on the Spiritual Assessment and Ideas for Action,
what can you do today to improve your focus?

Remember:
Analyze (reflect deeply)
Activate (determine an action item)
Accelerate (utilize your resources and strengths)

Steps and Rhythm

"First, we make our habits, and then our habits make us."

—JOHN DRYDEN

How are you today?

Have life responsibilities caught up with you yet?

Have you wanted to drift back into old habits?

As we embark upon a new week, be encouraged that just a few new steps each day will soon develop new rhythms, which will turn into new habits. Don't get too far ahead of yourself. Instead, simply focus on one day at a time.

Whether you are working on your personal or professional development today, remember to be mindful of disciplines which impact your progress. Consider making a vision board or cutting out pictures of your goals once they are achieved. How will you feel? What can you see? Then determine the steps and habits you will need to bring each goal into reality.

Often when we set new goals, we start off strong but soon go right back into our old daily motions, moving without thinking. Let's remember that we need to make positive changes in order to see positive results.

What small changes will you make today that will soon turn into new rhythms and new habits?

How can you visualize them and keep them in front of you for motivation and inspiration?

Who will inspire you to see beyond where you are right now?

One of the greatest attributes of God is that He can be our friend. Talk to him and tell Him how much you need Him as you make changes. Ask Him to be your #1 partner, your CEO and your friend. Ask Him to send others along who are stronger in areas where you are weak. Have confidence today that a good God cares about helping you make your life the best you want it to be. He sees and hears it all and He cares. Trust Him for the results.

Stop living life on automatic and step into the brand new you today.

IDEAS FOR ACTION:

- Go along your way differently today. Write one thing you can change in your daily routine that will lead to the accomplishment of your goals.

- Tell your accountability partner about this change.

- Commit to a new rhythm and be willing to accept the discomfort of doing something different. It will feel strange at first, and that is okay.

JOURNAL

Based on the Spiritual Assessment and Ideas for Action,
what can you do today to improve your focus?

Remember:
Analyze (reflect deeply)
Activate (determine an action item)
Accelerate (utilize your resources and strengths)

Your One and Only Life

Today is a great day, full of purpose!

In addition to our eternal salvation, which is the greatest gift we can receive from God, we also have the opportunity to believe that we are here on earth for a purpose. We do not have to see ourselves like any other person, just wandering through life, without direction. We can have meaningful, specific goals and actions to make an impact forever.

What if we lived every day like God was right there with us and He designed us to thrive?

Would we wake up with a pep in our step?

Would our to-do list be written out long before we went to sleep the previous day?

Would we move with purpose?

Would our desire increase to make our one and only life count for eternity?

Would we experience marked improvement in our daily productivity because we had something to look forward to?

Would the alarm clock be less of a nuisance?

Would the people around us sense our energy and pick
up their pace as well?

Don't skimp out on the one and only life you've been given. We don't get to do this again. This isn't a trial run. You are here, on purpose today, to do all God is calling you to do. What will you do with this gift you've been given called "life"?

IDEAS FOR ACTION:

- What could you do today to give yourself a "one and only life" mentality?

- Start planning a reward day or a trip for yourself. What goal must you meet in order to get there?

- If you aren't clear yet on why you are here, what your purpose is or how to live on purpose each day, please revisit chapter 6 of my book, *Grow with Goals, A How-to Guide for Activating Your Purpose.*

JOURNAL

Based on the Spiritual Assessment and Ideas for Action,
what can you do today to improve your focus?

Remember:
Analyze (reflect deeply)
Activate (determine an action item)
Accelerate (utilize your resources and strengths)

Grace-Full

---

*"Grace isn't a little prayer you say before
a meal. It's a way to live."*

–UNKNOWN

My encouragement today is to **KEEP GOING**.

Even if you have not been able to devote the time you desire to your goals yet, please know this:

You are NOT behind!

No matter where you are in the process of reaching your goals or where you think you SHOULD be, give yourself some grace. Grace means unmerited favor, pardon, and mercy. Even if you feel you don't deserve it, cut yourself some slack. You are empowered from this moment on to love yourself and not be hard on yourself. A good and loving God gave His one and only son so you could live free. He loves you!

Knowing you have been given grace makes it easier to give others grace too.

Today, step out of your past and into your present and future. I encourage you to change your perspective on your shortcomings, hindrances or areas of failure. Use them as lessons for learning. Ask God for His forgiveness. Forgive yourself and others who have stood in the way of your success.

As you forgive, you will make space in your heart and mind to let go of offense, bitterness and pain that is taking up room in your heart and your mind. When you release these shortcomings, you will make space to receive the new - new insights, new creativity, and new people to support and who will support you as you travel together through life's journey.

And then you will thrive in what you have set out to do!

IDEAS FOR ACTION:

- Love yourself and others today.
- Recognize there is no room for unforgiveness in your life.
- Make a plan to let go of the past hurts, habits and hangups that are holding you back.
- Repent where you have fallen short.
- Receive God's abundant love for you.
- Forgive yourself and determine your failures will become the stories that help others become free too.

JOURNAL

Based on the Spiritual Assessment and Ideas for Action,
what can you do today to improve your focus?

Remember:
Analyze (reflect deeply)
Activate (determine an action item)
Accelerate (utilize your resources and strengths)

Grateful Through and Through

"Gratitude is the healthiest of all human emotions."

—ZIG ZIGLAR

As we walk through each new day, we have many opportunities set before us. It's our duty to use wisdom as we select which opportunities to seize and which ones to let fall by the wayside.

> What will you choose?
> How will you choose?

Most of us have been blessed with so much, yet we often strive for more. While I believe in abundant lives full of more than we could ever ask or think, I also know the peace that comes when we rest in the goodness of what's already been given to us.

Today, make a covenant with yourself and God. A covenant that says no matter what I achieve or don't achieve, I am grateful simply for where I am with what I have. In your journal, write, sign, and date your covenant as a reminder to remain grateful and be gracious toward yourself in this journey.

See the sunrise and be grateful.

Listen for a laugh and be thankful.

Rejoice for your family, your car, and your bed.

Rejoice even in your sufferings.

Be thankful, knowing God causes everything to work together for the good for those who love Him and are called according to His purpose.

IDEAS FOR ACTION:

- Weigh your decisions today before you make them. Be wise! Eat well, write more, spend wisely, and work with a greater purpose in mind.

- Look around and listen for the small things. Make a list of blessings you notice today that you've never seen before.

- Before you hustle, thank God for the muscle. He can move any mountain you are facing!

- Be encouraged today with small steps. They make BIG differences.

- Before you go to sleep tonight, make a list of what you did well today.

- Before you fall asleep, decide that you will wake up proud of yourself tomorrow.

JOURNAL

Based on the Spiritual Assessment and Ideas for Action,
what can you do today to improve your focus?

Remember:
Analyze (reflect deeply)
Activate (determine an action item)
Accelerate (utilize your resources and strengths)

Follow-Through

"You are not stuck. You are being strategically positioned for this hour."

–GAIL MCWILLIAMS

Having goals takes courage. When you write your goal it declares to the ages, "This will be done." I believe the power of this declaration is the journey that grows our lives.

Be ready for trepidation when you make a declaration.

It's as if the forces of evil know you are soon to break through. They know you have spoken your intentions out loud. They know you mean business, and you will follow through. When we experience feelings of doubt, intense insecurity, and even physical discomfort, that is when we must press through the most.

You're almost through the end of your first week. Your week may have been full of momentum, or you may have been thrown some curve balls. Whatever the case, your mind is being transformed. I encourage you to break through, press through, and follow through.

This mission you are on, this goal you have declared, is bigger than you. The ripple effect of your changes will soon impact others. As that cycle continues, you may even start a movement. What you have declared could even change nations. Whether it's a health goal, a business idea, a purpose for your next investment, a fine-tuned career, or a new book—no matter what your goal is, it is part of a greater plan.

So, whatever your goal, get to it with peace. Put on your best armor in the midst of this battle and pour on the oil of gladness instead of mourning. You have the power to see from a new perspective today.

This week I have used overtly spiritual references because I believe everything starts in the spirit. I hope this week you have been enlightened and your spirit encouraged as we move forward in reaching our holistic goals.

IDEAS FOR ACTION:

- Keep declaring your goals. Share your "give up" goals and your "go up" goals with your accountability partner. You can revisit this concept in page 131 of my book, *Grow with Goals, a How-To Guide for Activating Your Purpose.*

- You may not know it yet because you are in the middle of the process, but the testing of your faith will soon result in gold.

- Continue to press through and follow through with a mind of calm and peace as well as intentional actions. Do not let anxiety, worry, fear, doubt, or discouragement set in.

- Go back to your list of how you plan to activate your goals. Are you following through on what you said you would do?

JOURNAL

Based on the Spiritual Assessment and Ideas for Action,
what can you do today to improve your focus?

Remember:
Analyze (reflect deeply)
Activate (determine an action item)
Accelerate (utilize your resources and strengths)

DAY 7

Success!

"Success is not a destination; it's a journey."

−ZIG ZIGLAR

You made it. I am so proud of you! It can be difficult to celebrate yourself, but please take a few moments today to look back on the GOOD, positive changes you are making. We can be so hard on ourselves when we don't execute a plan perfectly or when life happens, and we seemingly forget about our goals. I encourage you to have peace throughout this process. No matter what you did or didn't accomplish this week, I hope you are grateful for the opportunity, your bright mind, and the ability to push for more. Most of all, I hope you remember, a good God is with you and for you.

Sometimes we fail; don't be afraid of failure.
The more we fail, the more we learn.

Simply look at where you failed this first week of the journey. Then ask God for more grace and move on. Remind yourself that sometimes we fall short, and it's okay.

I'm sure you were busy this week. I'm sure you had things come up. I'm sure life threw you a couple of punches. Maybe you had relational difficulties, sales that didn't turn your way, resources that seemed low, or maybe your mind became cloudy, or your week was just a bit blah—no matter. You are not a failure. It's a new day and a new week ahead. Keep moving forward!

What is the best way to move forward? The secret is found in the positive choices we make daily.

I encourage you to put the pure, the positive, and the lovely in your mind today. What podcasts, music, or lessons are you hearing EVERY DAY? Listening to an encouraging and/or inspiring voice or music will raise your endorphins so you have the positive energy to make a change. Let's set ourselves up for another successful week.

IDEAS FOR ACTION:

- Today is accountability day! Share with your accountability partner the steps you made toward the goals you set this past week.

- Celebrate the small progress you've made.

- Use your journal!

- Take notice of bad habits you need to replace with good ones. What one bad habit can you replace next week?

- Find an encouraging voice to listen to and add that to your schedule.

- Hope for the harvest. You have been planting for many years. Your harvest is coming.

JOURNAL

Based on the Spiritual Assessment and Ideas for Action,
what can you do today to improve your focus?

Remember:
Analyze (reflect deeply)
Activate (determine an action item)
Accelerate (utilize your resources and strengths)

WEEK TWO

Physical Wholeness

GETTING INTO THE MINDSET OF TAKING CARE OF YOUR HEALTH

The first assignment for this week is to hold the most important meeting of the week: the *POWER meeting,* so you can determine the priorities and scheduling for the week. While it is different for everyone, and circumstances change from week to week, there are a few components to the weekly meeting that are necessary for success:

- Bring your calendar.
- Bring your current goals and needs for the coming week.
- Commit your week to each other and to God.

THE MOST IMPORTANT MEETING OF THE WEEK

WEEK OF ....

P PRAYER REQUEST

O OLD BUSINESS

W WHAT'S NEXT?

E EXPECTATIONS

R ROLES, RESPONSIBILITIES, AND RESOURCES

"The place of agreement is the place of power." Matthew 18:19

NIGHTLY BRAIN RELEASE - JOURNALING

My thoughts, ideas, concerns and worries

- ☐ ....
- ☐ ....
- ☐ ....
- ☐ ....
- ☐ ....
- ☐ ....
- ☐ ....
- ☐ ....
- ☐ ....
- ☐ ....

What is God saying about these items?

- ☐ ....
- ☐ ....
- ☐ ....
- ☐ ....
- ☐ ....
- ☐ ....

PRODUCTIVITY SCHEDULE

WEEK OF:

SUNDAY

G Y R   MY TOP 4 PRIORITY GOALS

G Y R

G Y R   ○ _____

G Y R   ○ _____

MONDAY

○ _____

G Y R   ○ _____

G Y R

G Y R

G Y R

TUESDAY

G Y R   THIS WEEK'S TOP THREE PRIORITIES, PROJECTS & PEOPLE

G Y R

G Y R   ○ _____

G Y R   ○ _____

WEDNESDAY

○ _____

G Y R

G Y R

G Y R

G Y R

THURSDAY

G Y R   IMPORTANT NOTES

G Y R

G Y R

G Y R

FRIDAY

G Y R

G Y R

G Y R

G Y R

SATURDAY

G Y R

G Y R

G Y R

G Y R

Weekly Focus

THE PHYSICAL SPOKE

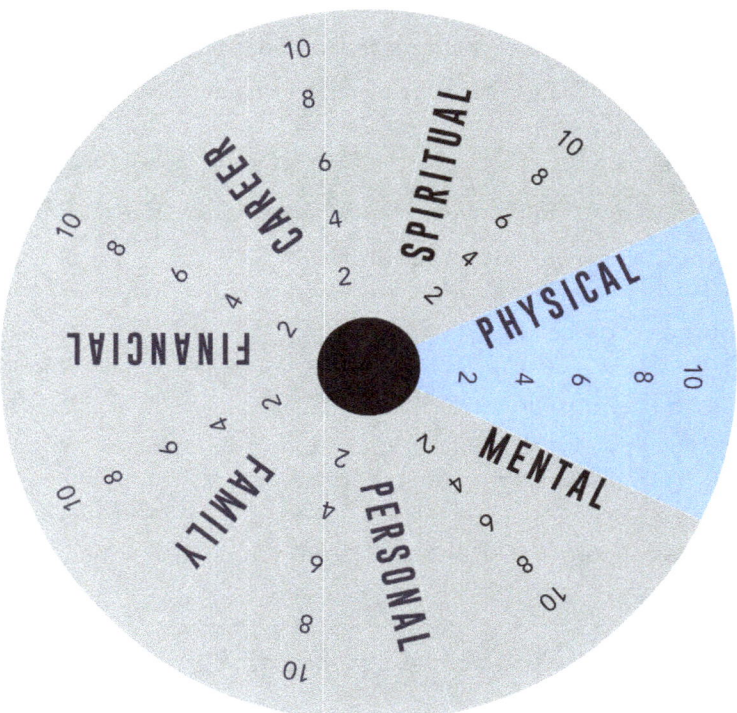

This is the start of a new week and the continuation of new habits. The goal of this week is to get you into the mindset of taking care of your health. Without a proper perspective of your physical health, you will not achieve all God has in store for you! If you are unhealthy, you will not be able to reach and fulfill your purpose. Or worse, you will burn the candle at both ends and experience burnout. I do not want this to happen to you.

I hope you are encouraged that the week ahead is full of promise as we focus on the Physical Spoke on our Wheel of Life!

On the next page is an assessment of the Physical Spoke on the Wheel of Life. Take your time and consider each question. Circle the answer that best reflects your current lifestyle.

Wheel of Life

PHYSICAL ASSESSMENT

Circle the answer that best reflects your current lifestyle.
Take the time to reflect on these.

YOUR CURRENT LIFESTYLE		YOUR SCORE				
1.	How would you rate your appearance?	1	2	3	4	5
2.	Do you get regular check-ups?	1	2	3	4	5
3.	How is your energy level?	1	2	3	4	5
4.	Do you have endurance and strength?	1	2	3	4	5
5.	Do you have a regular fitness program you stick to?	1	2	3	4	5
6.	How effectively do you control your weight?	1	2	3	4	5
7.	Do you eat a healthy and nutritious diet?	1	2	3	4	5
8.	How well do you control your stress?	1	2	3	4	5
9.	Are you free from indulgences and addictions?	1	2	3	4	5
10.	Do you get enough sleep?	1	2	3	4	5
11.	How do you feel overall physically?	1	2	3	4	5

Total: _____

Based on your score, what are the top four lifestyle changes you would like to work on this week? List those below.

This Week's Goals

FOR LIFESTYLE CHANGE IN
THE PHYSICAL SPOKE

GOAL 1	
GOAL 2	
GOAL 3	
GOAL 4	

What can you implement daily to increase this area of balance in your life? As you move through the week, consider the daily action items and how they relate to the four priority goals of improvement you have listed above. On the journal page, be sure to include the action items you have chosen and include your thoughts, fears, progress, etc.

Prioritizing Self Care

*"I hope that you may enjoy good health and
that all may go well with you,
even as your soul is getting along well."*

–THE BIBLE

Many years ago, the stress of life was weighing me down. I was diagnosed with adrenal fatigue, my hormones were unbalanced, I had no energy, I was depressed, and it showed in my physical health. In the years leading up to the diagnosis, I went through two miscarriages and experienced significant weight gain.

I wasn't taking care of myself. I had too much going on. I was too busy with work, life and my family to prioritize myself. Maybe you've felt like I did. I knew I needed to make big changes, but I wasn't sure how. So, I started small.

This pattern seems to be a regular occurrence in my life. In order to feel better and live longer, I often must adjust my work rhythms. Some of the things I know to do include protocols that have worked for me including taking time for breathing, scripture meditation, stretching, essential oils, prioritizing skincare, scheduling regular dental care, annual doctor visits, and nearly daily physical exercise. I have a long way to go, but even though I am not perfect, I have broken the cycle of neglecting myself. Over this second week, I will discuss in more depth what has helped this high achieving woman, who loves work, to prioritize wellness.

How do we prioritize our physical health and self-care? There is so much good knowledge and information available to us today. But as we determined on day one, we are following this journey with the tree of life in mind, rather than the knowledge of good and evil. Knowledge isn't enough. Many of us may know the answers, but we often fail to put them into action. We make physical wellness a priority by scheduling it in our calendars and sticking to our plans. Many of us have physical goals, and we WILL get there! Together we will.

Let's start small and not try to tackle this problem all at once.

This week, consider one thing that has helped me immensely: waking up at the same time every day. Let's begin to implement a consistent practice of taking care of ourselves.

IDEAS FOR ACTION:

- Identify physical goals for your life and add them to your journal.
- Wake at the same time each day to begin the process of getting circadian rhythms in place.
- Write your top priorities for this week. Remember to keep your physical health as important as your other goals.

JOURNAL

Based on the Physical Assessment and Ideas for Action,
what can you do today to improve your focus?

Remember:
Analyze (reflect deeply)
Activate (determine an action item)
Accelerate (utilize your resources and strengths)

My Health Journey

*"Do you not know that your body is a temple
of the Holy Spirit, who is in you,
whom you have received from God? You are not your own;
you were bought at a price. Therefore, honor God with your body."*

–THE BIBLE

For much of my adult life, I have struggled with my weight. Chalk it up to DNA, menopause, perimenopause and having babies. You name it, I think my body has been through it.

When I was younger, I thought that good physical health was about how I looked on the outside. My primary focus was working out and eating right. My insecurity about my body led me to do things so I wouldn't get fat. I ran daily, completed multiple races, including 5Ks, 10Ks, a triathlon, and a half marathon. I've gone over 6 months without sugar, tried every diet on the planet, hired personal trainers and read many books on the topic. With every weight loss attempt and so much good information, I was being changed on the inside, and even developing good habits I put into action; however, my primary focus was still trying to reach a certain image on the outside. I admit, there was a lot of vanity.

But everything changed when I turned 40. Two weeks before my 40th birthday, I had my first miscarriage. After giving birth to three healthy children, I was in total shock that something was so wrong with my body that I could not carry my pregnancy to full term. (I realize our physical health is not the only reason we have miscarriages. There are times in life when this just happens. These are the times when we must trust in a divine purpose and plan with our children and with infertility.)

I continued to soldier on, and a year later, I became pregnant again. At that time, I was being treated for fatigue; my body was burned out. I wasn't sleeping well, often waking in the middle of the night for hours at a time. I was going to a wonderful women's health doctor who treated me with things I needed, like Vitamin B12 shots and supplements to help calm my overworked brain. I was treated for food allergies, vitamin deficiencies, and hormone imbalance, and it seemed to be going well, but then I had another miscarriage. Despite the many positive changes that I made, my doctor and I both knew that even more significant things needed to change in my life. I was stressed, and my body was letting me know. I began to take my health much more seriously, making every effort to get healthy in my body and in my mind, and that included counseling.

While I am being open with you, most people around me did not know these things were going on. I was living a normal life, giving my best at work every day, taking care of my family, and going about my daily activities. Maybe you've been there. If you have, my heart goes out to you.

My closest friends and family knew I was not myself, and the toll stress was taking on me began to show in everything I did.

During this time, I began getting into a lot of little car accidents I call "bump ups." I wasn't hitting others, thank God, but I was hitting everything else…the mailbox, a couple of little walls, many a curb. It became humorous.

Until it wasn't. I was short-tempered and became bothered by the smallest things. I was late all the time. My closet was a disaster; I just didn't have the physical energy to even hang up my clothes. I would often stay up late into the night, binge watching stupid shows, just to escape the struggle in my mind. All these became signs that something wasn't right with me. I wasn't myself anymore.

Have you ever felt this way? Can you relate? I hope not. You may be younger than me and haven't necessarily had to be concerned with your health yet. Or you may be older and have similar stories. No matter where you are today, I hope my story serves as a reminder that we need to take care of our bodies so we can be at our best and do all we are created to do with our one and only life.

But we can't do it alone; I need help in this area often! Ultimately, I came to find that I was missing a little hormone that was causing anxiety, stress and resulting in miscarriage. I needed this hormone on board to complete a pregnancy while also being in perimenopause. I'm thankful to my doctor that we made adjustments, and I was able to have a healthy baby girl when I was 42. She is truly a planned miracle that came out of lot of partnership with my doctors.

Good partners for our health journey are a must. We all need a "Health Success Team." My mother is a nurse, so she is my first go-to. I used to hate going to doctors, but she has helped me find both good traditional physicians as well as holistic solutions. I had to put my trust in these people's hands to get me on the right track! For years now, I have had an endocrinologist and a professional counselor, and I take supplements as part of my daily rituals.

I now know what is needed and although my health is still a work in progress, my mindset has changed. I now take my health seriously and view my body from a very different perspective

> What's your story?
> What do you need to do to focus on in your health?
> Are there medications or supplements you need to add or doctors
> you need to consult?
> Are addictions holding you back?
> Do you need to adjust your life pace?

Please remember, we want you to live a long and healthy life. Our bodies do not belong to us, and when we pass away, we will no longer need them. But they have been given to us on loan to steward well. I think one of the most important things to remember is to give ourselves grace during different seasons of life. Ultimately, some of our health is out of our control. Women and men both go through different seasons in our life journey; we will have ups, and we will have downs. Let's stay challenged and consistent as best we can.

IDEAS FOR ACTION:

- Write or think about your health journey beyond just your weight and your external image. How are you doing on the inside? Are there indications that maybe you are not living your healthiest life?

- Are there rhythms you can change and steps of action you can take to help?

- Think about your "Health Success Team." Who is helping you become the healthiest you can be? Make sure you have trusted advisors to help you measure and assess your physical health.

- Do you have an exercise regimen? If you don't, start small: touch your toes in the shower. Drink your water. Go for a walk or jog at lunch. Do 20 push-ups. Today, do something to move and get your blood pumping!

JOURNAL

Based on the Physical Assessment and Ideas for Action,
what can you do today to improve your focus?

Remember:
Analyze (reflect deeply)
Activate (determine an action item)
Accelerate (utilize your resources and strengths)

DAY 10

Sweet Dreams

"A good laugh and a long sleep are the best cures in the doctor's book."

−IRISH PROVERB

How are you sleeping? Don't skip over the question; really think about resting habits and sleep.

Why is it important to talk about sleep?

Sleep has become very important to me. Part of the story I shared with you yesterday–and a contributing factor to my physical challenges–has been erratic sleep patterns. One of the greatest indicators of stress is not sleeping well, so if you are having trouble falling or staying asleep, start noticing the patterns. As you know by now, rest is extremely important to achieving our goals. If we aren't getting proper rest, our relationships are strained, our performance on the job weakens, our tempers are shorter, and sleeplessness opens the door to sickness.

According to the Center for Disease Control, "Sleep is increasingly recognized as important to public health, with sleep insufficiency linked to motor vehicle crashes, industrial disasters, and medical and other occupational errors. Unintentionally falling asleep, nodding off while driving, and having difficulty performing daily tasks because of sleepiness may contribute to these hazardous outcomes. Persons experiencing sleep insufficiency are also more likely to suffer from chronic diseases such as hypertension, diabetes, depression, and obesity, as well as from cancer, increased mortality, and reduced quality of life and productivity. Sleep insufficiency may be caused by broad-scale societal factors such as round-the-clock access to technology and work schedules but sleep disorders such as insomnia or obstructive sleep apnea also play an important role. An estimated 50-70 million US adults have a sleep or wakefulness disorder."

> Do you have a difficult time going to sleep?
> Are you waking up in the middle of the night?
> Are you tossing and turning?
> Is your performance affected because you are not getting enough sleep?

If you are having any trouble sleeping, talk about it. My hope is that you will not have to rely on something to make you sleep but that you will lay your head on your pillow and rest, going to bed with peace each evening and waking up with joy each morning. Years ago, I found a checklist online that helped me settle down before going to bed.

I used this checklist for many months. It helped me download all of my thoughts from the day onto one sheet of paper. Perhaps you write in a journal or write things in your calendar before bedtime, or maybe you have a specific routine you follow each night. Whatever your system–try to monitor your activities before you go to bed and visualize the great things that are going to happen for you the next day.

IDEAS FOR ACTION:

- Complete the Get Sleep Checklist at https://www.webmd.com/sleep-disorders/your-sleep-checklist.

- Which one of these checklist items do you like best? Check it out and get some sleep!

- In alignment with our 3 Part Productivity System, keep completing the brain release before bed each night. Write all that's on your mind. Release this information out of your subconscious so you can rest.

JOURNAL

Based on the Physical Assessment and Ideas for Action,
what can you do today to improve focus?

Remember:
Analyze (reflect deeply)
Activate (determine an action item)
Accelerate (utilize your resources and strengths)

The Fasted Lifestyle

"Fasting is more than a moment; it's a lifestyle."

–JILL HELLWIG

I want you to accomplish and achieve all you set out to do during this 40 days, this year and the rest of your life. You have begun with momentum and there is nothing that can hold you back! There may be obstacles that come your way, but you can move through them with grace and peace because, in the midst of the process, you remember that all things will ultimately work together for your good. Be tenacious and remember why you are doing this. You only get one life and you are determined to live it on purpose. Whatever your assignment is in this current season, you have the tools and skills you need for where you are today.

How do we stay on track and ensure our daily decisions are the right ones? I have found that living a lifestyle of fasting is the best way for me to learn to deny my physical desires and stay in tune with my Creator. This practice turns my inner critic into a positive inner voice.

Many people have found fasting to be a rewarding spiritual experience. I want to also talk a bit about the physical benefits of fasting. I believe the two experiences (both spiritual and physical) go hand in hand.

Don't stress about embarking on an extended fast. Some people have completed 40-day or 21-day water fasts, and if you sense you should do that, I support you and urge you to seek your doctor for any direction.

Instead, consider living a fasted lifestyle, abstaining from food a certain meal every week, or a regular day every week. I have found this practice helps with my spiritual development as well as cleansing and purifying my physical body. Fasting gives our bodies a moment to take a time out from digestion and eating to reset what is going on inside. I believe fasting gets us closer to our Creator, clarifies our purpose and helps us understand our master design. It also gets our bodies in a mode of healing themselves.

Desire and Appetite.

We live in a world that is about satisfying our appetites. No matter what we want, our world tells us to get it and to have more of it. Our physical desires and fleshly human bodies crave; we crave food, we crave fun, we crave acceptance. We crave money, security, love, pleasure….and the list goes on and on.

How beneficial would it be if we learned to say "no" more often and learned to curb our hunger?

Denying myself and my desires has proven to be the path to getting back to what really matters, to get my mind and body back into alignment with the right cravings. In the past, I've done fasts from 1 to 10 days.

Over the years, I've committed to living a fasted lifestyle. For me, that has taken on different forms. Sometimes it looks like not eating food on Mondays. I've fasted sugar, flour, soft drinks and more. For you, it may mean something completely different, but I'd like you to consider the concept of fasting regularly for added spiritual, health, and life benefits. Don't let this become another rule you have to follow, but something you choose. This should be a spirit-led activity in which you feel complete freedom to give up all food or some food (maybe sugar, meat or bread). The rhythm and length of the fast are completely up to you.

These words touched me, and I hope they will speak to you too.

> "Once the primary focus of fasting is firmly fixed in our hearts, we are at liberty to understand there are also secondary purposes in fasting. More than any other discipline, fasting reveals the things that control us. This is a wonderful benefit to the true disciple who longs to be transformed. We cover up what is inside us with food and other good things, but in fasting these things surface. If pride controls us, it will be revealed almost immediately. Anger, bitterness, jealousy, strife, fear - if they are within us, they will surface during fasting. At first, we will rationalize that our anger is due to our hunger, then we will realize that we are angry because anger is within us. We can rejoice in this knowledge because we know that healing is available through the power of Christ."
> – Richard Foster, Celebration of Discipline[1]

IDEAS FOR ACTION:

- Consider your fasting schedule for the remainder of this 40 Day journey. How can you implement the concept of living a "fasted lifestyle"?

- What appetites, desires, or cravings control you? Can you identify them? Consider fasting as a means to live life beyond your human desire.

- Can you see how fasting can help you reset and realign your goals?

- What do you think about fasting, and what's your plan? How will you continue this concept throughout the year? Write your thoughts.

JOURNAL

Based on the Physical Assessment and Ideas for Action,
what can you do today to improve your focus?

Remember:
Analyze (reflect deeply)
Activate (determine an action item)
Accelerate (utilize your resources and strengths)

Persistent Consistency

> *"The fastest way to success is to replace*
> *bad habits with good habits."*
>
> –TOM ZIGLAR

I once had the privilege of hearing Tom Ziglar (Zig Ziglar's son) speak at a workshop about his health journey. When I was working for Tom years earlier, he decided to change his diet by only eating what was pure. He felt the pure and the positive were aspects of his mental life, so he needed to pull them into the area of his physical health as well.

Tom began buying all organic food, eating nothing that wasn't "made by God." It worked for him, and over time he lost more than 60 pounds, which he has kept off for over a decade.

Tom attributes his success to something he calls "persistent consistency." Every day, no matter how he felt or what his schedule was, regardless of whether he was traveling, he made an appointment with himself in the morning. He made sure his workouts were early and effective, and he hired a personal trainer to help keep him on track. He started grocery shopping and cooking with his wife and perfected a wonderful homemade salsa recipe to keep his food interesting. He was consistent in his efforts over a long period of time, and he saw incredible results. He was persistent in the face of obstacles, pain, and weariness, and, in the end, he found success.

Think about this concept for a moment. Have you applied persistent consistency to your goals?

> Are you tenacious to a fault?
> Are you engaged daily in the battle?
> Are you riding a roller coaster where some days you get results while other days you feel more like a failure?

We can all learn from this concept. Remember what John Dryden says, "First we make our habits, and then our habits make us." This applies in every area of life, especially the physical.

IDEAS FOR ACTION:

Evaluate yourself on a scale of 1 to 5, with 5 being "all the time" and 1 being "almost never."

- How effective are you at remaining persistent in spite of obstacles?

- How consistent is your daily routine?

- As you consider your health and physical well-being, how can you apply persistent consistency to your daily ritual? Get up the same time every morning? Set alarms when it's time to eat? Schedule your workouts on your calendar? Find a partner or coach to help you stay on track?

I applaud you for what you've already done and the changes you're already making! We all know the tortoise won over the hare. Just a little every day keeps our momentum going and our pace flowing.

JOURNAL

Based on the Physical Assessment and Ideas for Action,
what can you do today to improve your focus?

Remember:
Analyze (reflect deeply)
Activate (determine an action item)
Accelerate (utilize your resources and strengths)

The Path of MOST Resistance

---

*"Taking the path of most resistance often
leads to the most reward."*

−ANN VOSKAMP

We are coming to the end of week two. I hope your week has been successful. Most likely, it's been busy, but you are actively pursuing your goals, and that means you live a full life. I hope you are basking in the richness of that fullness.

We have all heard of the Path of Least Resistance. It seems to be the natural path our bodies want to take. For example, hikers often choose the easiest way to cross over a steep incline. It seems to be a wise thought, as it preserves energy and helps us work in a way that is "smart but not hard."

The path of least resistance is a scientific theory as well. Wikipedia (don't they know it all?) says this:

"The path of least resistance is the physical or metaphorical pathway that provides the least resistance to forward motion by a given object or entity among a set of alternative paths. The concept is often used to describe why an object or entity takes a given path. For example, water always flows downhill, regardless of whether briefly flowing uphill will help it gain a lower final altitude (with certain exceptions). In physics, this phenomenon allows the formation of potential wells where potential energy is stored because of a barrier restricting flow to a lower energy state."

This is an interesting concept to study. I think most of my life, I would have agreed—and in certain situations, I still do—that the path of least resistance helps us to maximize our energy, time, and talent to produce a good result. But not always.

The hard things often give us the most reward. In parenting. In physical fitness. In our health. In writing. In marriage. In our studies. In working with difficult people. In our finances.

It is in the hard things, the difficult moments, the adversity, and the staying when it's tough, pushing through and walking up that steep mountain where we get the most reward. Our muscles grow, our lungs expand and when we get to the top, we can see further, taking in the most beautiful views. If we can find it in ourselves to push and challenge our bodies, our result is almost always better.

As much as I love the summit, life isn't just about those mountaintop experiences. It's about the tough hike to the top and what we glean and see along the way. How much more effective will we be when we overcome fear, laziness, difficult conditions, and our own limiting beliefs to make the right choices every day?

These tough decisions move us toward our goals and push us to stretch beyond our comfort zones. This applies to physical activity and more, and I hope it gives you a new perspective—to hike higher, push further, and go beyond your physical limits to do more than you ever thought you could. Let's make our muscles sore today.

And when we get there, oh, when we get there, what a joyous day that will be! We will so proud of ourselves for pushing through.

- Take the path of MOST resistance today. Try doing one activity in a new way and journal how it goes.

- Do you have a habit of taking the path of least resistance in physical activities? For instance, do you prefer the elevator over taking the stairs? Do you opt for fast food over the task of preparing a home-cooked meal?

- What are the least resistance paths you can set aside today to begin developing habits that require more effort, more attention, and more healthy gains?

JOURNAL

Based on the Physical Assessment and Ideas for Action,
what can you do today to improve your focus?

Remember:
Analyze (reflect deeply)
Activate (determine an action item)
Accelerate (utilize your resources and strengths)

Time to Celebrate!

*"Life is a journey, and the key to a happy journey
lies in celebrating each step along the way."*

-RICHARD CARLSON

I hope you have identified some significant triumphs during the past month that will keep your momentum flowing for the rest of the year and keep you focused on setting the RIGHT goals forever.

As we discussed in chapter 6 of *Grow with Goals, A How-To Guide For Activating Your Purpose*, you have a unique purpose, calling, and assignment and the gifts you've been given are irrevocable. Bad decisions, difficult circumstances, or unfortunate pieces of our lives are not the end of the story. There is a time for everything. A time to mourn and a time to cry. A time to be born and a time to die. And there is a time to celebrate.

I love celebrations. I absolutely love celebrating my husband and my kids' birthdays. Over the years, I have loved throwing them birthday parties, writing them special notes, buying their cakes, sharing pictures and giving them words of affirmation.

I love celebrating extended family and friends. I love sending cards and finding the perfect gift, which is a reflection of a milestone achieved or a moment to be remembered. Parties, holidays, streamers, games and singing are my sweet spot. I love it all!

One celebration I especially love each year is celebrating the anniversary of our church. Our family is one of the founding families who helped plant Create Church with Pastors Ryan and Ellie Binkley and an amazing Dream Team in Richardson, Texas on January 26, 2014.

Each year, we have a beautiful celebration of all that has happened since the birth of the church. This is one of my favorite days to look forward to at the beginning of each year. It isn't really about balloons, cake, cookies and more. I love celebrating how far we've come, all of the people who have been along for the ride and the lives that have been impacted. I also love it because our church anniversary is just one month ahead of our daughter's birthday. So, every time we celebrate an anniversary at the church, I compare it to our daughter's development, and it brings me great joy to see God's promises revealed right before my eyes.

> What can you do today to celebrate something you've done so far in this journey?

We all have opportunities in our lives to celebrate milestones. Some people go through life thinking and saying, "It's no big deal." Well, you know what? I think you're a big deal and the little changes you're making, barriers you're breaking, and hope you're dealing, are making a positive impact on yourself and the world. I acknowledge your work in this and want to affirm you in your efforts. I'm so proud of you!

I hope you will be mindful to celebrate and take extra moments to reward yourself for a job well done. Continue in awe, with a grateful and expectant heart for all that is ahead.

Keep going this week, and you will see your life transform right before your eyes!

IDEAS FOR ACTION

- Today is accountability day. Share with your accountability partner the steps you made toward the goals you set this past week.

- Celebrate the small progress you've made.

- Record your progress in your journal.

- Look back on the last two weeks. If you haven't already, focus on your achievements.

- Celebrate, be grateful, and live with a renewed sense of direction and purpose as we keep moving forward.

JOURNAL

Based on the Physical Assessment and Ideas for Action,
what can you do today to improve focus?

Remember:
Analyze (reflect deeply)
Activate (determine an action item)
Accelerate (utilize your resources and strengths)

Client Success Story

THE ENCOURAGER

When asked how many years it took for me to write my book, my response has been 73 years. I can assure you that without Jill Hellwig's help, it would have taken many more.

Jill has a unique gift to see through complexities directly to the core of what is needed. Then with a few simple, properly placed, encouraging words and tips, she coached my book, *FEROCIOUS LOVE*, right out of me.

Since then, she has become a vital team member with our non-profit organization. She has contributed many no-nonsense insights that have unlocked and resolved challenges to our progress. Her strategic vision and consultations with our team have helped to expand our reach around the globe. As of the date of this writing, we have reached over 160 million people with the image of the Lion of Judah.

We are so grateful to Jill for keeping us on track and continually moving forward so we can achieve our mission of being a non-profit global collaboration of believers offering the love of Jesus to every person on earth through an encounter with the Lion of Judah.

Latimer Bowen
Project7billion.org

WEEK THREE

Mental Wholeness

CHALLENGING YOUR MINDSET TO EARN THE BEST REWARDS – PEACE, JOY AND LOVE

The first assignment for this week is to hold the most important meeting of the week: the *POWER meeting,* so you can determine the priorities and scheduling for the week. While it is different for everyone, and circumstances change from week to week, there are a few components to the weekly meeting that are necessary for success.

- Bring your calendar.
- Bring your current goals and needs for the coming week.
- Commit your week to each other and to God.

THE MOST IMPORTANT MEETING OF THE WEEK

WEEK OF ....

P
PRAYER REQUEST

O
OLD BUSINESS

W
WHAT'S NEXT?

E
EXPECTATIONS

R
ROLES, RESPONSIBILITIES, AND RESOURCES

"The place of agreement is the place of power." Matthew 18:19

NIGHTLY BRAIN RELEASE - JOURNALING

My thoughts, ideas, concerns and worries

☐ ....

☐ ....

☐ ....

☐ ....

☐ ....

☐ ....

☐ ....

☐ ....

☐ ....

☐ ....

What is God saying about these items?

☐ ....

☐ ....

☐ ....

☐ ....

☐ ....

☐ ....

PRODUCTIVITY SCHEDULE

SUNDAY

_____ G Y R

_____ G Y R

_____ G Y R

_____ G Y R

MONDAY

_____ G Y R

_____ G Y R

_____ G Y R

_____ G Y R

TUESDAY

_____ G Y R

_____ G Y R

_____ G Y R

_____ G Y R

WEDNESDAY

_____ G Y R

_____ G Y R

_____ G Y R

_____ G Y R

THURSDAY

_____ G Y R

_____ G Y R

_____ G Y R

_____ G Y R

FRIDAY

_____ G Y R

_____ G Y R

_____ G Y R

_____ G Y R

SATURDAY

_____ G Y R

_____ G Y R

_____ G Y R

_____ G Y R

MY TOP 4 PRIORITY GOALS

○ _____

○ _____

○ _____

○ _____

THIS WEEK'S TOP THREE PRIORITIES, PROJECTS & PEOPLE

○ _____

○ _____

○ _____

IMPORTANT NOTES

Weekly Focus

THE MENTAL SPOKE

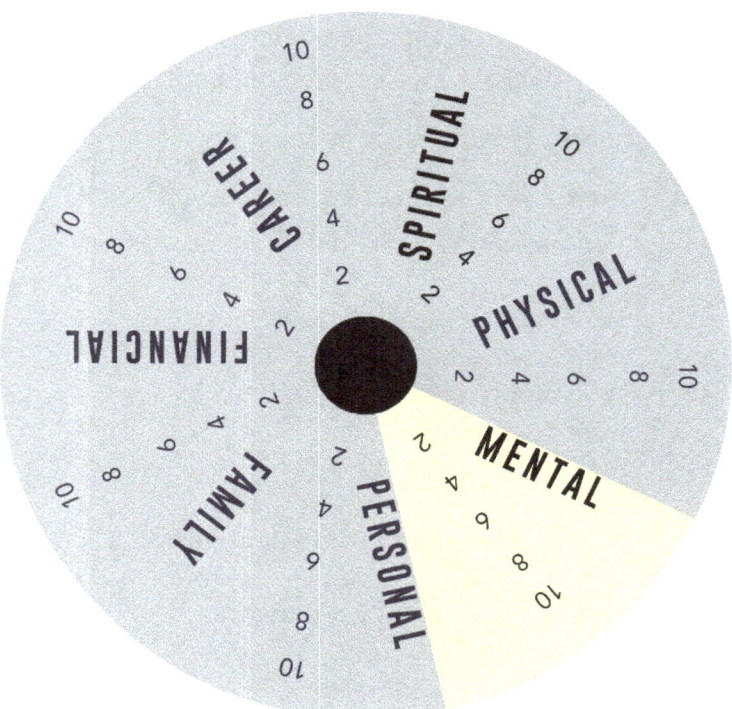

This week, we are focusing on our mental health and our mental goals, both of which begin with loving ourselves. So many of us go through life working to obtain the external factors of success: earning money, buying a new home, wearing the best fashion, traveling to exotic places, building a great business, etc. However, those who earn the best rewards – peace, joy, and love – have the healthiest minds. Let's challenge your mindset to the brand new you.

Part-way through the week, we hit the halfway point of our 40-day journey! Congratulations. Keep moving forward.

On the next page is an assessment of the Mental Spoke on the Wheel of Life. Take your time and consider each question. Circle the answer that best reflects your current lifestyle.

Wheel of Life

MENTAL ASSESSMENT

Circle the answer that best reflects your current lifestyle.
Take the time to reflect on these.

YOUR CURRENT LIFESTYLE	YOUR SCORE				
1. How would you rate your overall mental health?	1	2	3	4	5
2. How would you rate your intelligence?	1	2	3	4	5
3. What formal education have you completed?	1	2	3	4	5
4. Are you emotionally intelligent?	1	2	3	4	5
5. Are you using your creativity and imagination?	1	2	3	4	5
6. How much time do you set aside for ideation, invention, and creativity?	1	2	3	4	5
7. Do you participate in continuing education (online classes, podcasts, classes, books, etc.)?	1	2	3	4	5
8. How inquisitive are you?	1	2	3	4	5
9. How healthy is your self-image and outlook on life?	1	2	3	4	5
10. Have you overcome areas of trauma and loss to continue moving forward?	1	2	3	4	5
11. Do you struggle with anxiety, depression, or reactive behavior?	1	2	3	4	5

Total: _____

Based on your score, what are the top four lifestyle changes you would like to work on this week? List those below.

This Week's Goals

FOR LIFESTYLE CHANGE IN
THE MENTAL SPOKE

GOAL 1	
GOAL 2	
GOAL 3	
GOAL 4	

What can you implement daily to increase this area of balance in your life? As you move through the week, consider the daily action items and how they relate to the four priority goals of improvement you have listed above. On the journal page, be sure to include the action items you have chosen and include your thoughts, fears, progress, etc.

Benchmarks and Milestones

"Inch by inch, life's a cinch. Mile by mile, it's a trial."

–JUDY HENNING (MY MOM)

My mom is one of the most positive people I know. She is a happy encourager to so many people, a ready support who sees the good. I admit, sometimes I can see the glass as half empty or as Dennis Prager says, I can look at a ceiling and see only the missing tile. Sometimes, I get stuck in my head with what is wrong and then I know it's time to call Mom. Her sweet and positive voice is soon celebrating some little thing I did, or one of my kids did, and I'm always in awe how she rejoices at what sometimes could seem the simple and mundane. But those little progressions in life are what make it great.

Great medicine for our mental health is to acknowledge our simple blessings and celebrate our mundane achievements! Knowing we have succeeded puts a pep in our step and a smile on our faces. Soon, we begin framing our lives with positivity and can see the good.

About three years after I first began implementing my own coaching and goal setting process, I decided to teach others what I was doing. I taught my first class on goal setting and then sent the class an email each day for forty days. The emails I sent were the beginning of this book.

In the middle of that process, early one morning, I knew it was going to be a great day. Before jumping into my day, I stepped on the scale and weighed myself. I could not believe my eyes. The number before me was one I hadn't seen since giving birth to my youngest child. I had been fighting for two years to get the baby weight off and couldn't get below a certain number—and then it happened. No longer did I weigh in one bracket. I was in another. I may have only lost 4 ounces since the day before, but that 4 ounces had a big impact on my state of mind.

This was a milestone marker I had hoped to reach in a certain amount of time, and I was so grateful it was achieved a little early. I soon had another milestone set to reach by the end of the next month, and it encouraged me to keep the momentum going.

Little by little, I made my way toward the goal. It wasn't one big leap; it was a series a little productive steps.

And the same thing happened with writing this book. It was just a series of little benchmarks achieved over time that allowed this entire milestone to come together.

> What about you?
> Have you passed any milestones on the path to your goals this month?

If so, then take a moment and whoop and holler like I did that morning! If you can't find the good, maybe it's time to call Mom. It might not be your mom or mine, but find an encouraging voice who helps you put in perspective all the effort you're putting in.

I hope you are breaking your big goals into manageable pieces so you can accomplish a little each day. This makes the journey much more fun because you can reward yourself for progress and start seeing your dreams move into reality.

Inch by inch, life really is a cinch. And mile by mile, it becomes a trial. Keep the momentum going today toward all your goals!

IDEAS FOR ACTION:

- Is there a small and/or significant benchmark you achieved this month? If so, celebrate it!

- If you haven't identified milestones for your goals, begin to think about some today. Let your accountability partners know what they are, so they can celebrate with you as you achieve them.

JOURNAL

Based on the Mental Assessment and Ideas for Action,
what can you do today to improve your focus?

Remember:
Analyze (reflect deeply)
Activate (determine an action item)
Accelerate (utilize your resources and strengths)

DAY 16

Ac-Cent-Tchu-Ate the Positive

"You've got to accentuate the positive. Eliminate the negative. Latch on to the affirmative. Don't mess with Mister In-Between."

–JOHNNY MERCER

Mental goals start with renewing our minds every day. Renewing our minds requires inputting the pure and the positive.

What are you listening to each day?

What is your self-talk?

What words are you speaking?

VAIN IMAGINATIONS AND LIMITING BELIEFS

Too many times, our minds are filled with vain imaginations, worry, fear, or negative self-talk. Vain imaginations are thoughts about us and what others think of us. These thoughts can become strongholds and idols if we are not careful.

They can limit our ability to think clearly about a situation and create open doors for deception. Thoughts full of worry, fear, or negativity will also limit us from doing all we are Called by God to do. We wouldn't allow someone to throw garbage in the middle of our home, would we? Then why would we do that to our own minds?

TAKE OUT NEGATIVE, PUT IN POSITIVE

Rather than thinking about those things (whether we are good enough, have what it takes, what others think, how we can never do something, if we have enough resources, etc.), we need to renew our minds daily, and sometimes hourly, by replacing that mindless chatter with pure and positive self-talk.

I like to listen to podcasts, worship songs, sermons, and more.[2] I find that when I hear positive words, they add another dimension to reading them. While reading engages our intellect, listening aligns our emotions. Both are vital in the process of renewing our minds.

When I miss this type of encouragement, I literally crave it. It's as though my mind knows what it needs.

Is your mind craving positivity? **Let's begin today!**

IDEAS FOR ACTION

- Measure your thoughts.
- Measure your self-talk.
- Measure your words. What are they producing?
- Share with your accountability partner your favorite positive voices. Whom do you listen to the most? We all need valuable resources.

JOURNAL

Based on the Mental Assessment and Ideas for Action,
what can you do today to improve your focus?

Remember:
Analyze (reflect deeply)
Activate (determine an action item)
Accelerate (utilize your resources and strengths)

Your Fine Mind

"As a man thinks, so he is."

–THE BIBLE

Determining mental goals is about developing our fine minds. Whether you believe you are intellectually superior or intellectually challenged—you are correct. In fact, our beliefs, our thinking, and our meditations have more to do with our reality than anything else.

In a day when we have access to abundant knowledge at our fingertips, at any time of day, we must remember it is not just knowledge that matters, but it's also the way we apply that knowledge. Turning our positive thoughts into action is how we differentiate ourselves to achieve our goals.

To stay positive, unclutter your mind from the toxic messages coming from this world.

How long as it been since you engaged your creativity?
How long has it been since you let your imagination soar?

Take some time today to clear your mind from all the clutter. Doodle, draw and dream.

Sit down and read a good book to give you inspiration or listen to a good book to get you moving. Find what inspires you and see yourself as a continual learner.

Eric Hoffer says this, "In times of change, learners inherit the earth, while the learned find themselves beautifully equipped to deal with a world that no longer exists."

Change can be tough, and our world is changing rapidly. Think about what a creative, intelligent and excellent learner you are. And ask God, the most creative of all, to guide you with inspiration, creativity and insight into reaching your goals. I have no doubt your great mind, partnered with Him, will come up with unique solutions as you make your world, and all of ours, a better place.

IDEAS FOR ACTION

- Share your results of the assessment of the Mental Spoke from the Wheel of Life with your accountability partner. Talk about how difficult or easy it was to complete this assessment.
- Think about how your mental health affects the goals you have set for this program. How can you improve one of these 11 areas to help you reach your goals?

Keep learning!

JOURNAL

Based on the Mental Assessment and Ideas for Action,
what can you do today to improve your focus?

Remember:
Analyze (reflect deeply)
Activate (determine an action item)
Accelerate (utilize your resources and strengths)

The Value of Counseling

*"Ours is not the task of fixing the entire world
all at once, but of stretching out to mend the part
of the world that is within our reach."*

—CLARISSA PINKOLA ESTES

Whether you scored 55 on the Mental Spoke assessment or an 11, there are times when we need more encouragement and help than we can provide for ourselves. Today we will discuss the value of therapy and mental health counseling.

Many of us want to make a difference and play a significant part in this world. If you didn't want that, you probably wouldn't be reading this book, and there is great merit to that mindset. To be the difference-makers we were born to be, we need to first work through the trauma and pain of our past and the hidden issues within. Only then can we extend a hand of healing to those who need our story and can be reached by the difficulties of our own life.

Some experiences like trauma, abuse, conflict, and loss are not ones we can handle or get through on our own. In order to keep moving forward, and to keep going with our goals, we need to mend our insides first.

Professional counseling is an excellent way to do a "tune-up" for your mind and emotions. Just like you need to tune up your car and get oil changes, we also need to "tune-up" our hearts and our minds and "check under the hood" to be sure everything is running smoothly.

Different from coaching, counseling helps us work through deep layers of bitterness, problems we find unsolvable, grief, pain, anger, unforgiveness, and more. Counseling also takes the pressure off our spouses and our closest family and friends. Instead of constantly rehashing our thoughts with those we love most, we can release our innermost thought patterns to a professional who knows how to help us make sense of it all. The benefit is that we keep our closest relationships from being unduly strained or exasperated while also gaining another perspective from a wise source.

My desire is for you to live with peace, joy, and love as you have never experienced before. I believe good counseling is a vital step in the process of achieving mental freedom.

IDEAS FOR ACTION

- Consider areas of trauma, loss, abuse, grief, or pain. Have you sufficiently worked through them, so you are completely mended from the inside out?

- Even if it hurts to bring up difficult feelings buried deep inside, consider how processing these thoughts and emotions with a wise counselor can help you move to another level.

- Your inner child is begging you to get healed from the pain. You are loved and there is hope. Start the process today to search for a trusted therapist. For a list of resources, please see my website, www.brandnewu.org

JOURNAL

Based on the Mental Assessment and Ideas for Action,
what can you do today to improve your focus?

Remember:
Analyze (reflect deeply)
Activate (determine an action item)
Accelerate (utilize your resources and strengths)

You're Braver than You Think

"There is no normal life that is free of pain. It's the very wrestling with our problems that can be the impetus for our growth."

−FRED ROGERS

Tomorrow is halfway into our 40-Day program!

What strides have you made?
Have you noticed any changes?

I cannot congratulate you enough on moving toward your destiny.

The ideas for action from yesterday's reading were heavy and may have left you feeling shaken.

Use your set-aside time today to revisit any areas of hurt or difficult emotions. Keep digging deeper to recognize and mend these areas through self-care.

If you were prompted yesterday to consider seeing a counselor, take steps today to put that into motion. Talk to your accountability partner about your decision and ask them to help you pray about finding the right counselor.

You are halfway there! It's all downhill from here! Continue through, follow through, and keep going. Receive these words deep into your heart, soul and mind today:

"Promise me you'll always remember: You're braver than you believe, and stronger than you seem, and smarter than you think." - Christopher Robin from Winnie the Pooh

IDEAS FOR ACTION:

- Take time to catch your breath and catch up where you can.

You are not behind. You are right on time!

JOURNAL

Based on the Mental Assessment and Ideas for Action,
what can you do today to improve your focus?

Remember:
Analyze (reflect deeply)
Activate (determine an action item)
Accelerate (utilize your resources and strengths)

Gold Level Living

"Stay Steady. Faithfulness has its rewards. Don't quit yet!"

–JILL HELLWIG

You've made it halfway through our 40-Day goals journey, and I am so proud of you.

As we persist toward our goals, following through on our daily tasks, giving our best in our lives and at our jobs, and as we labor and plant, we develop the beautiful quality of faithfulness.

Throughout my life, I have learned that faithfulness has its rewards. We aren't sure where and we won't know when, but I can promise that our acts of faithfulness will be rewarded.

Let me give you an example. Years ago, we were given second-row tickets, floor seats, to a Dallas Mavericks NBA basketball game. What an experience! We saw the players on the court, had a four-course meal, took in the sights and sounds of the American Airlines Center, and were ushered into "gold level" underground parking.

The game became a special moment in time–not the pinnacle of life, but a sweet double date night with our dear friends Daisy and Steven Greek. Throughout the night, we kept reminding each other of the onus of "gold level living." When a big basket was made or maybe when we met someone famous, or even saw ourselves on the big screen, it became a fun mantra, "Here's to gold level living." We had a really fun night in a season where the four of us each needed some encouragement that when we are faithful, surprises will come our way. Since that time, probably seven or eight years ago, every time we see or talk to the Greeks, we wink and smile big and ask each other how we're coming along on our goal of "gold level living."

It tells us in scripture, when we get to heaven we will walk on streets of gold, but can you believe and hope with me for "gold-level living" here on earth too? These next 20 Days are going to be a broadening of our horizons to see further, think bigger, and reach for more than we could ever fathom. There is gold being discovered right in front of our eyes.

Be encouraged as we keep pressing to Day 40.

You WILL come forth as gold!
I believe it. Do you?

IDEAS FOR ACTION:

- Recount God's faithfulness in your life over these last 20 days. Be grateful for the harvest coming from the seeds you have planted.

- Make a new commitment to yourself to stay committed. Share your resolve with a friend or your accountability partner to not only help you stay on track, but to encourage them that they too can have gold level living.

Most people start to taper off when they get to the middle of something, but that's not you. Stay focused and consistent until the completion of this program and watch your life be transformed.

I believe in you! You can finish strong and step into the brand new you

JOURNAL

Based on the Mental Assessment and Ideas for Action,
what can you do today to improve your focus?

Remember:
Analyze (reflect deeply)
Activate (determine an action item)
Accelerate (utilize your resources and strengths)

Examine Your Environment

"Go where you are celebrated, not just tolerated."

– BOB BEAUDINE

Did you know people possess some qualities similar to plants? Why yes, they do! Both plants and humans are living organisms that need water to live and thrive. While plants need sunlight and carbon dioxide to keep them living, humans need calories and oxygen.

Some of us are like hearty ferns and some of us are similar to delicate orchids. The environment we need for sustenance, growth, and health will be as different as our personalities, strengths, and needs as individuals and families.

No matter what type of plant we are, whether we are a fine aged redwood or a long-growing bamboo, we need to be planted in a setting that will provide the nourishment we need to thrive.

> Do the habitats in which you dwell breed confidence in you as a person?
> Or do they zap your life and stunt your growth?
> Do your surroundings reflect your value as an individual?

Or does the ambiance where you reside, work, or live make you want to wilt and die?

Whether it is your home, your place of work, your friendship and family circles, or any other environment where you spend a lot of time, we need to identify the qualities that are most life-giving and literally breathe life and confidence into us.

Then we can become our best. When you've made important environmental changes, you'll be in a place where you are not only receiving life, but you are giving it too. You will be living your best, most confident, and self-assured life. And you will leave others feeling their best too.

IDEAS FOR ACTION:

- Today is accountability day! Share with your accountability partner the steps you made toward the goals you set this past week.

- Celebrate the small progress you've made.

- Use your journal.

- Take notice of bad habits you need to replace with good ones. What one bad habit can you replace next week?

- Find one new encouraging voice to listen to and add that to your schedule.

- Hope for the harvest. You have been planting for many years. Your harvest is coming.

- Write it. What environment do you think you thrive most in?

- Look at your current environments. Do you need to make some environmental changes? If so, you can! Get around like-minded people, places, and programs. The ability to reach your goals is up to you.

I believe in you and look forward to seeing how your life will flourish as you begin to root in healthy, life-giving environments.

JOURNAL

Based on the Mental Assessment and Ideas for Action,
what can you do today to improve your focus?

Remember:
Analyze (reflect deeply)
Activate (determine an action item)
Accelerate (utilize your resources and strengths)

WEEK FOUR

Personal Wholeness

GETTING INTO THE MINDSET OF BEING ALIVE WITH PASSION

The first assignment for this week is to hold the most important meeting of the week: the *POWER meeting*, so you can determine the priorities and scheduling for the week. While it is different for everyone, and circumstances change from week to week, there are a few components to the weekly meeting that are necessary for success:

- Bring your calendar.
- Bring your current goals and needs for the coming week.
- Commit your week to each other and to God.

THE MOST IMPORTANT MEETING OF THE WEEK

WEEK OF..

P PRAYER
REQUEST

O OLD
BUSINESS

W WHAT'S
NEXT?

E EXPECTATIONS

R ROLES,
RESPONSIBILITIES,
AND RESOURCES

"The place of agreement is the place of power." Matthew 18:19

NIGHTLY BRAIN RELEASE - JOURNALING

My thoughts, ideas, concerns and worries

- [ ] ....
- [ ] ....
- [ ] ....
- [ ] ....
- [ ] ....
- [ ] ....
- [ ] ....
- [ ] ....
- [ ] ....
- [ ] ....

What is God saying about these items?

- [ ] ....
- [ ] ....
- [ ] ....
- [ ] ....
- [ ] ....
- [ ] ....

PRODUCTIVITY SCHEDULE

WEEK OF:

SUNDAY

G Y R
G Y R
G Y R
G Y R

MONDAY

G Y R
G Y R
G Y R
G Y R

TUESDAY

G Y R
G Y R
G Y R
G Y R

WEDNESDAY

G Y R
G Y R
G Y R
G Y R

THURSDAY

G Y R
G Y R
G Y R
G Y R

FRIDAY

G Y R
G Y R
G Y R
G Y R

SATURDAY

G Y R
G Y R
G Y R
G Y R

MY TOP 4 PRIORITY GOALS

○ _____
○ _____
○ _____
○ _____

THIS WEEK'S TOP THREE PRIORITIES, PROJECTS & PEOPLE

○ _____
○ _____
○ _____

IMPORTANT NOTES

Weekly Focus

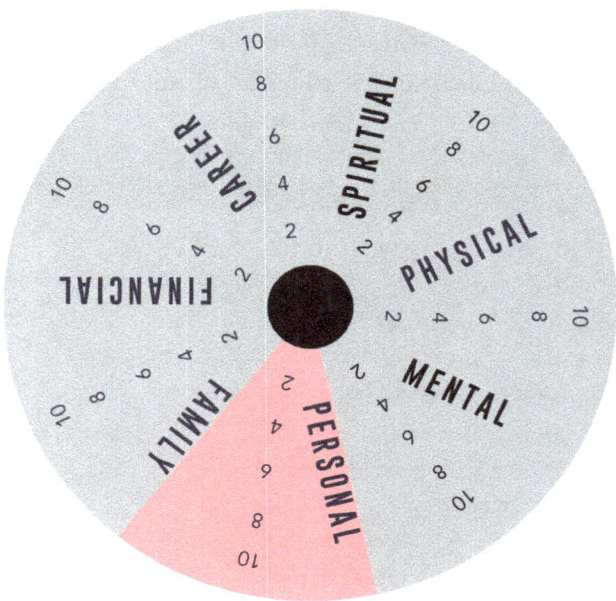

In addition to coaching you toward your goals, my primary focus for this 40-day journey is to help produce healthy individuals. This is why the first four weeks we covered the areas needed for your own personal development:

- Week One: Spiritual (becoming aligned with your purpose)
- Week Two: Physical (taking care of your vessel)
- Week Three: Mental (thinking about the right things)

For week four, we cover the Personal Spoke, which makes us alive with passion. Then we can move on to the other spokes of the wheel that impact how we influence the world around us, including family, finances, and career.

Let's see what we can do to set goals toward discovering and living out our passion in week four!

Next is an assessment of the Personal Spoke on the Wheel of Life. Take your time and consider each question. Circle the answer that best reflects your current lifestyle.

Wheel of Life

PERSONAL ASSESSMENT

Circle the answer that best reflects your current lifestyle.
Take the time to reflect on these.

	YOUR CURRENT LIFESTYLE	YOUR SCORE				
1.	How often do you set aside time for recreation?	1	2	3	4	5
2.	How often do you exercise?	1	2	3	4	5
3.	What's the state of your relationships?	1	2	3	4	5
4.	How frequently do you participate in community activities?	1	2	3	4	5
5.	Do you participate in service clubs?	1	2	3	4	5
6.	How often do you keep a regular solace/quiet time?	1	2	3	4	5
7.	How often do you set aside time for growth?	1	2	3	4	5
8.	Is your life consistent?	1	2	3	4	5
9.	Do you use social media appropriately?	1	2	3	4	5
10.	How is your time management?	1	2	3	4	5
11.	How fulfilled do you feel in your personal time?	1	2	3	4	5

Total: _____

Based on your score, what are the top four lifestyle changes you would like to work on this week? List those below.

This Week's Goals

FOR LIFESTYLE CHANGE IN
THE PERSONAL SPOKE

GOAL 1	
GOAL 2	
GOAL 3	
GOAL 4	

What can you implement daily to increase this area of balance in your life? As you move through the week, consider the daily action items and how they relate to the four priority goals of improvement you have listed above. On the journal page, be sure to include the action items you have chosen and include your thoughts, fears, progress, etc.

Moments of Truth

Webster's definition:
"A time when a person or thing is tested,
a decision has to be made,
or a crisis has to be faced."

When I worked for Zig Ziglar, we taught customer service training to major companies, government entities and organizations around the world. One of the techniques we spent time on was the concept of *Moments of Truth*. Within every client experience are several opportunities where an organization has a chance to make an impact or impression. Good or bad, these moments make an experience unforgettable—either in a helpful or a detrimental way.

These moments come in every interaction: first impression, handshake, phone call, website, marketing, sales transaction, follow-up, and after-the-sale service.

Moments of Truth are important because the interactions we have with our clients have the power to turn them into raving fans and advocates for our business success or the opposite.

Moments of Truth are vitally important now, as customers and potential customers have the ability to make or break an organization on social media, Google and Yelp reviews, and more.

I include a link in the notes section if you want to read more about *Moments of Truth*[3] on why client experience is so important today. If you are a business owner, this is an important idea for you and your employees to know and practice.

**I believe today represents a moment of
truth between you and me.**

Moments of Truth aren't just limited to customer service but happen in our personal lives as well.

We've been going along this program for 22 days now. This is the start of a new week.

- Some of you are doing great, and I applaud you!

- Some of you are feeling overwhelmed, and I still applaud you!

- Some of you may think you're a failure, but I want to remind you that you are not failing. Failure is an event; it is not a person. And I still applaud you!

- And some of you may wish you could be as good as all the other people following through in this program. Stop that right now. There is only one you. You don't have to compare yourself. And I still applaud you!

Today is your moment of truth. Today you have a moment to make a commitment to yourself:

**Either commit to the next 18 days to achieve your goals,
or fail to commit because you are too far behind.**

You may have skipped some days or missed some daily habits and made some bad decisions. You may be right on track. You may think you are too busy to keep up with all this. (I've thought and done all these things).

Here are some ideas I hope will set you free:

- If you have had some aha moments and realize you didn't set the right goals when you first started, crumple up those goals and start again with the right goals this time. It's not too late.

- Maybe you need to start smaller and make it easier on yourself.

- Maybe you need to start bigger and s-t-r-e-t-c-h yourself more.

- How about starting with one goal this week that you have to work to achieve, but that will give you the greatest results?

- Maybe you realize you want to have more fun, and you didn't set a goal for that. You can make this fun. This is your life, after all!

Remember, my greatest desire is for you to complete this program with the tools to set the right goals aligned with your truest inner desires, your core values, and your purposes in life. (If you haven't done this yet, I suggest going through my book, *Grow with Goals,* to discover these beautiful assets of who you are.)

Today is your *Moment of Truth*, and I believe you can do it. I push because I want to see you do great things.

IDEAS FOR ACTION:

- Get out your calendar **right now** and plan our week.

- Write your **priorities** for each day.

- Rewrite or adjust any goals you need to begin again. Dream bigger or start smaller—make adjustments as needed but be sure you can **measure your results.**

- Launch out some new goals in the areas where you are least balanced on your Wheel of Life.

- Live with purpose and priority this week.

JOURNAL

Based on the Personal Assessment and Ideas for Action,
what can you do today to improve your focus?

Remember:
Analyze (reflect deeply)
Activate (determine an action item)
Accelerate (utilize your resources and strengths)

Let's Get Personal

"The earth has its music for those who will listen."

–GEORGE SANTAYANA

The Personal spoke of the wheel is the spoke that makes you come alive!

This week we continue working on our personal growth and development; as we do so, we can begin to think higher with even greater perspective.

This will be a fun week as we dream a little bigger and give our goals some payoff. This process should release you to be ALL you are and live the life you love.

The challenge from yesterday about the *Moments of Truth* brought the opportunity for reflection and commitment to move forward. Use your set-aside time today to revisit any areas where you may be struggling or losing interest in moving forward.

Dig deep to uncover any feelings of fear, frustration, or failure that may be trying to keep you from finishing the next 17 days. Talk to your accountability partner if you feel the urge to run or the temptation to walk away from this journey before reaching the finish line.

- Look back at Day 5, Grateful Through and Through. Recommit to the covenant you made with yourself for this 40-day journey. A covenant that says no matter what you achieve or don't achieve, you are grateful simply for where you are and what you have.

- Make a new playlist, find an inspiring new song. Belt it out or dance along.

- Remain grateful and keep moving forward.

JOURNAL

Based on the Personal Assessment and Ideas for Action,
what can you do today to improve your focus?

Remember:
Analyze (reflect deeply)
Activate (determine an action item)
Accelerate (utilize your resources and strengths)

Get Clothed in Confidence

"When a person of purpose walks into a room, clothed in confidence, compelled by compassion, and anointed with discernment, there is no force on earth that can keep them from shifting the atmosphere!"

–JILL HELLWIG

I hope you have had the chance to rate yourself in the Personal Spoke on the Wheel of Life. If you haven't, do it now!

We can set the rights goals, align them with the right priorities, and have peace every day. But if we don't have the confidence to get it, we will leave things on the table. This little word—this "c" word of confidence—is where all the difference is made.

In Hebrew, the word for confidence is a "strong tower of trust." In Greek, confidence means freedom.

> I want you to have so much confidence in the divine plans and purpose for your life that you have no fear or worry that you are not enough.

I want you to have so much freedom in being who you are that you can walk into any room and make a difference by being yourself.

I want you to have so much trust in a good God who created you that you will follow His Call and do All he has destined for you since the beginning of time.

IDEAS FOR ACTION:

- Think of ways you hold yourself back through your insecurities and lack of confidence.

- What adjustments can you make to increase your confidence levels?

- Do you equate introversion or shyness with a lack of confidence? You can be confidently outgoing, engaging, and friendly, even if you are an introvert.

- This confidence will draw others to you and create an energy about you that will not only make your goals become reality, but you'll also be making a difference in the lives of others.

Commit to increasing your confidence today!

JOURNAL

Based on the Personal Assessment and Ideas for Action,
what can you do today to improve your focus?

Remember:
Analyze (reflect deeply)
Activate (determine an action item)
Accelerate (utilize your resources and strengths)

DAY 25

What to do When Conflict Arises

"You cannot change what you are not willing to confront."

–JAY HELLWIG

I hope your confidence is building every day. I hope you are stepping out, doing more, reaching further, and going beyond what you imagined was possible. Wherever you found yourself when you started this journey, I hope you find yourself in a better place today—one where you are pushing forward while practicing contentment.

So, what do we do when conflict arises?

Conflict comes in circumstances not going as expected, and in relationship trials, difficulties, clashes, disputes, and disagreements. One of the greatest conflicts we can experience is feeling "conflicted."

Internal conflict is bad territory as it keeps us from pushing forward in freedom. Feeling conflicted often arises when we are worried about the expectations of others more than we are concerned about what God thinks about our issue and our own well-being and goals. Being conflicted is also a result of our values not being aligned with an action we are taking. We may be missing the mark, and we know it.

When you feel conflicted, check your motives and who you are trying to please. You will be sure to find something that is out of alignment.

Remember, the most important person to please is God and simple acts of obedience lead us closer to Him. Keeping this important fact in mind will keep our Personal Spoke of the Wheel healthy. Keeping our values in line with our actions will also help us create long sustaining relationships with others because they know who we are, and they will be able to trust us. We are walking in integrity when we are not conflicted inside. We are in alignment with ourselves.

Conflict looks entirely different when it is external. We can be assured that when we are pushing toward our goals, we have an opponent that wants to do anything in his power to keep us from our goal of mastery, including creating conflict and division. It is extremely important to recognize this and remain locked into truth. This truth states that we are not warring against flesh and blood (people) but against powers of darkness. This perspective helps us recognize conflict for what it is—an attack to make us falter.

Sometimes conflict comes in the form of miscommunication, as a result of outside pressures, or from simply being tired. When we recognize the conflict for what it is, we can either fall into the trap of offense or remain in a place of peace.

I wish I could say I have no conflict, but that's simply not true. Over the years, I've come to realize that when I am in conflict with others, I can't be my best self. There are times when conflict paralyzes me or, even worse, it makes me retreat from my goals.

What about you?

Sometimes we simply will not see eye to eye with someone, but we can learn to address disagreement head-on. We can be mature and secure individuals by working through difficult issues with others. Sometimes issues are resolved, and sometimes, they are not. When given an opportunity for resolution, we can be grateful and extend forgiveness. When things cannot be resolved (irreconcilable differences), we must move forward without feeling constantly conflicted or driven by this emotional pain. We must get healing and let go.

I'm writing about this because it helps us to expect conflict and to remember if we can move through it, we can learn to pursue our passion and purpose with a higher perspective.

I hope your days of conflict are few, and even more, I hope you are not conflicted inside.

This is getting personal—let's strive to balance those roller-coaster emotions to ensure we are happy, healthy, and pursuing our goals.

IDEAS FOR ACTION:

- Assess your comfort with conflict. Do you avoid it or move through it maturely and securely?

- In what ways can you make conflict your friend?

- Are you believing for a particular conflict to be resolved? Tell your accountability partner and share your hopes with them about this.

- Have you allowed conflict to hinder you from reaching your goals? Has it paralyzed you or even made you retreat? Reconsider the role this could play in your life. How can you adjust, get healing where needed and keep moving forward?

JOURNAL

Based on the Personal Assessment and Ideas for Action,
what can you do today to improve your focus?

Remember:
Analyze (reflect deeply)
Activate (determine an action item)
Accelerate (utilize your resources and strengths)

What's Your Reward?

"When we experience feelings of awe, it strengthens our sense of well-being and also makes that moment last longer."

—HAPPIFY

You are moving forward and making steps toward your positive future. I'm so proud of you!

Now that you are making headway, I have a question to ask, "How will you reward yourself for your progress?"

Our lives should be fun!

As we bring our goals into reality, Zig Ziglar says we move from survival to stability, from stability to success, and from success to significance.

Each stage in this process of life should become more enjoyable and rewarding. We no longer worry only about daily survival. We begin to have more and an overflow from which we can experience greater things. Eventually, we have more than enough so we can give back and do more to help others. This freedom makes all the hard work worth it.

We don't have to wait until we have achieved a certain level in order to give right now and reward ourselves for achieving good things.

A gift we can give ourselves is a break from work for rest and recreation.

The wisest man who ever lived, Solomon, told his followers that there is a time for everything, and that to find enjoyment in life is to find a good thing. I know many of us are high achievers who genuinely love work and are looking to go further and do more. But are you stopping to ENJOY the fruit of your labor?

What brings you the greatest joy?
Do you enjoy extra time with your family?
Is it traveling that you love?

Is it a hobby like photography, horseback riding, crafting, or shopping?
What is that thing or those things that tickle you and make you laugh?
How long has it been since you were in AWE?

How long has it been since you had a WOW moment?
When was the last time you looked at something with AWE and savored the moment?

If it's been a while, take the time to reward yourself.

Break down your goals into smaller steps and reward yourself at each level. Goals don't have to be big, but make sure at every micro goal reached, you acknowledge your effort.

Can you reward yourself soon? What goals have you completed in this journey? Plan to gather some friends and celebrate together. These don't have to be expensive events; focus on creating meaningful moments to remember how far you've come and to help you stay on track as you continue moving forward.

IDEAS FOR ACTION:

- Make a detailed plan of the tasks needed to complete your goals.

- Set small rewards in the middle of your goal reaching that keep you on track and give you moments of inspiration and pure joy.

- If you're serious about work and don't play a lot, think about ways you can make yourself relax and increase your well-being.

- Embrace the fun side of life! Laugh every day! Play every week! I give you permission!

When you're having fun, those around you will be too. Then watch what happens as that fun turns into even more goals achieved. Go enjoy your life, my friends. It's the only one we have!

JOURNAL

Based on the Personal Assessment and Ideas for Action,
what can you do today to improve your focus?

Remember:
Analyze (reflect deeply)
Activate (determine an action item)
Accelerate (utilize your resources and strengths)

Yes, She Just Went There!

"Love is an ice cream Sunday, with all the marvelous coverings. Sex is the cherry on top."

–JIMMY DEAN

TO MY SINGLE FRIENDS:

I firmly believe sex is best, most fulfilling, and most sacred when saved for your husband or wife. I remember times of singleness (I wasn't married until I was 27) when I longed to feel loved and wanted to be close and feel the affection of another. Sex isn't the answer, however.

Stay true to your purity, stay focused on living the life you love and keep pursuing the presence of Christ. You may have times of loneliness, but that happens in marriage, too, so wait for the right one. Grace will overwhelm you as you stay true to yourself and allow God to be your spouse during your season of singleness.

I love the story of Ruth. As she worked in the field, she was fulfilled in her life. She was a pioneer who would not leave her closest ally, her mother-in-law. Together, they accomplished much for the Lord. Their legacy was in the lineage of Christ.

Imagine all you can do as you stay focused on your current season at hand. Married or not, you are more than enough! You are worthy of love, affection, and attention. Find ways to connect with other Go Getters. Serve alongside friends. Take this time to experience amazing journeys and vacations, with or without others.

You are a powerful, anointed child of God, and you are not alone!

TO MY MARRIED FRIENDS:

Sex or internet access - which do you prefer?

Did you know that a recent study of over 2,100 adults in a Lithium sponsored Harris poll found that 48% of us would give up good sex before taking away internet access? [4]

Well, that's a sobering thought - no internet access or no sex. Which would you choose? The choice may not be that easy!

How's your sexual well-being?

Sex is as important for our well-being as good nutrition. It's also an indicator that our "happy hormones" are working and our life, in general, is in balance. When we lose a desire for sex, it can be an indicator that something else is going on. I believe we were made to thrive.

There are times when intimacy is slowed down or even stopped because of health issues, menopause, reduced libido, aging, pregnancy, grief, and more. In these times, we can be fulfilled in a loving relationship with our partner based on mutual understanding, loving commitment, and friendship.

Emotional intimacy is just as import as physical intimacy. To create a more fulfilling marriage, studies show it also gives more confidence, a greater sense of well-being, and happiness. Connection is what matters most.

So, my message to you is this: if the intimacy in your marriage isn't fulfilling or active, consider the possible reasons why. If this is a difficult topic for you because of abuse, trauma or difficult past circumstances, I direct you to seek a counselor who can help you work through the pain.

What is holding you back?

> Do you have internal struggles, past pain, or health issues?
>> Is your spouse going through something you need to know about?
>>> Is your lack of desire for intimacy a reflection of something more going on in your relationship?
> Could one of you have a sexual addiction (unusual focus or impulsive need for sex)?
>> Or have you simply let life get in the way and need to be more intentional in this area?

Make it your mission to have good, fulfilling intimacy with the spouse of your youth. Why?

An important gift we can give to our spouse and ourselves is health and vitality in this area.

IDEAS FOR ACTION:

- Tell your spouse how attracted you are to them, how much you admire them, and show them your affection. Don't withhold any good thing from them. If you don't have the desire you once had, consider getting help from a trusted doctor, therapist or friend. Something might be going on physically or emotionally you need to identify. There is no shame in this. It is a normal stage of life for many people.

- Recognize sexual needs and sexual seasons. Be in tune with your spouse's needs as well as your own. Is there a health challenge, additional stress in your life, or something keeping you from enjoying this area of your personal life?

- Seek emotional intimacy with your spouse, not just physical intimacy. Connect with them regularly about what you need to be freer and more fulfilled in this area.

- Seek help. Whether it is professional counseling, your doctor or a health practitioner, remember you have been created to have enjoyment in this area of life.

JOURNAL

Based on the Personal Assessment and Ideas for Action,
what can you do today to improve your focus?

Remember:
Analyze (reflect deeply)
Activate (determine an action item)
Accelerate (utilize your resources and strengths)

Sit Back, Relax, and Enjoy!

"You were designed for accomplishment, engineered for success, and endowed with the seeds of greatness."

–ZIG ZIGLAR

Can you believe you have already completed four weeks of this program?

Today is the last day we focus on the Personal Spoke on our Wheel of Life. Instead of giving you more information today, I give you permission to sit back, relax, and enjoy this day.

Stop.

Breathe.

Hope.

Repeat.

As you pursue your goals for years to come, this slowing down to appreciate what you've accomplished will be the most critical ingredient to your future success. Be grateful for where you are. Put into practice the art of enjoying being you. You, my friend, are the only you there is. Give yourself grace today as you rest in God's provision for you.

IDEAS FOR ACTION:

- Take time to journal your thoughts. Write down what you did well this week. Focus on the good and celebrate your successes.

- Go outside and breathe air deep into your lungs. You are alive!

- Take a walk and notice the sky. You are not in control of everything, and that is okay. Rest and feel assured.

- Enjoy just being.

- Today is accountability day! Share with your accountability partner the steps you made toward the goals you set this past week.

- Celebrate the small progress you've made.

- Take notice of bad habits you need to replace with good ones. What one bad habit can you replace next week?

- Find one new encouraging voice to listen to and add that to your schedule.

- Hope for the harvest. You have been planting well. Your harvest is coming.

JOURNAL

Based on the Personal Assessment and Ideas for Action,
what can you do today to improve your focus?

Remember:
Analyze (reflect deeply)
Activate (determine an action item)
Accelerate (utilize your resources and strengths)

The year 2018 was a turning point for me! It was time to do something drastic. Little did I know it would lead to some of the most powerful decisions and steps that still resonate with me to this day.

For years, I walked with others in casting vision, identifying goals, and seeing them meet their personal and professional milestones. For some reason, I was stuck. This led me to a conversation with Jill Hellwig that morphed into hiring her as my Executive Coach, getting unstuck and making a plan. I was in for a major "aha" moment!

The life changer wasn't simply about the objectives or targets; it was about who I wanted to become while pursuing my goals. Looking at the "wheel" seemed overwhelming, until I narrowed my focus on my 4 main goals: dramatic weight loss, give my best to my bride, purchase our first home, and build a sustainable business. It was quite the journey realizing each of these seven milestones and pushing through the setbacks, challenges, and even disappointments leading up to each celebration; yet I stuck to the plan and focused on the small steps versus the big leaps!

Fast forward, I lost significant weight and became healthier, my bride and I spent more quality time with new adventures and travels, we built our first dream home together, and the business idea continues to evolve. I still use these steps when I need to shift focus or realign my personal or professional vision and focus. It works!

Recently, I was chatting with Jill, and we both took a step back to honor what God did then and now as my wife and I get to work from our home, the very same home we prayed over years ago and made the decision to add as a goal. Our home is our sacred space and allows us quality time together. The seeds planted years ago are still growing and thriving years later. The plan works!

I still stand by the concept that goals are simply words on paper until you activate and put hands and feet to them each day consistently! Wherever you are, keep pursuing and choose progress over perfection. You're built on purpose, for purpose, with purpose! It's GO time!

Expect the best!
Joshua R. Ortiz

WEEK FIVE

Family Wholeness

GETTING INTO THE MINDSET OF REALIZING THAT COMING TOGETHER AS FAMILY IS PRIORITY

The first assignment for this week is to hold the most important meeting of the week: the *POWER meeting,* so you can determine the priorities and scheduling for the week. While it is different for everyone, and circumstances change from week to week, there are a few components to the weekly meeting that are necessary for success:

- Bring your calendar.

- Bring your current goals and needs for the coming week.

- Commit your week to each other and to God.

THE MOST IMPORTANT MEETING OF THE WEEK

WEEK OF ....

P PRAYER REQUEST

O OLD BUSINESS

W WHAT'S NEXT?

E EXPECTATIONS

R ROLES, RESPONSIBILITIES, AND RESOURCES

"The place of agreement is the place of power." Matthew 18:19

NIGHTLY BRAIN RELEASE - JOURNALING

My thoughts, ideas, concerns and worries

☐ ....

☐ ....

☐ ....

☐ ....

☐ ....

☐ ....

☐ ....

☐ ....

☐ ....

☐ ....

What is God saying about these items?

☐ ....

☐ ....

☐ ....

☐ ....

☐ ....

☐ ....

PRODUCTIVITY SCHEDULE

WEEK OF:

SUNDAY

G Y R
G Y R
G Y R
G Y R

MONDAY

G Y R
G Y R
G Y R
G Y R

TUESDAY

G Y R
G Y R
G Y R
G Y R

WEDNESDAY

G Y R
G Y R
G Y R
G Y R

THURSDAY

G Y R
G Y R
G Y R
G Y R

FRIDAY

G Y R
G Y R
G Y R
G Y R

SATURDAY

G Y R
G Y R
G Y R
G Y R

MY TOP 4 PRIORITY GOALS

○ _____
○ _____
○ _____
○ _____

THIS WEEK'S TOP THREE PRIORITIES, PROJECTS & PEOPLE

○ _____
○ _____
○ _____

IMPORTANT NOTES

THE FAMILY SPOKE

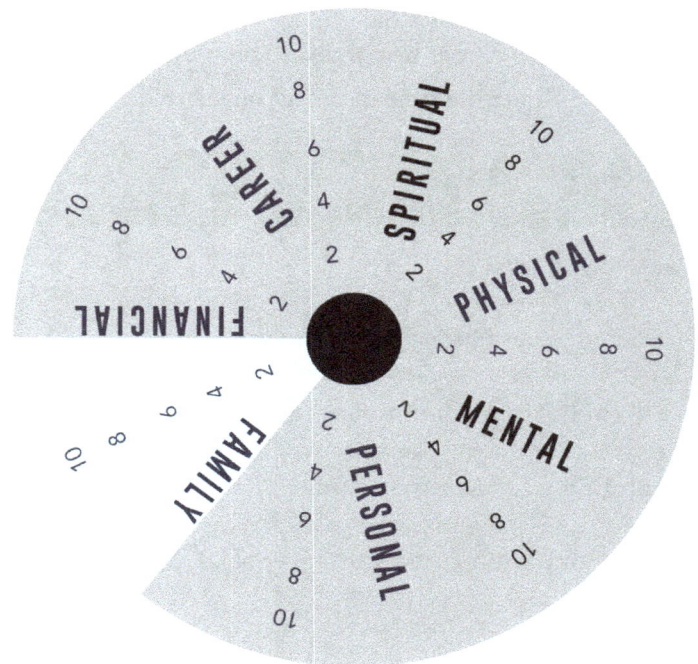

Earlier in my career, I worked for 14 years at the Zig Ziglar Corporation. At the beginning of every week at the Ziglar Corporation, staff and guests would start the week with devotions. This is a 30-minute meeting set aside for an inspirational speaker to encourage us to start our week with God. Mr. Ziglar called this meeting "the most important meeting we will hold in our company this week."

Each week he was in town, he sat on the front row, taking notes as a student, learning from others, despite the fact he was the "great Zig Ziglar!" He often said, although there would be big deals closed during the week, strategy meetings internally and with clients, this simple commitment to come together was the priority.

On the next page is an assessment for the Family Spoke on the Wheel of Life. Take your time and consider each question. Circle the answer that best reflects your current lifestyle.

Wheel of Life

FAMILY ASSESSMENT

Circle the answer that best reflects your current lifestyle.
Take the time to reflect on these.

	YOUR CURRENT LIFESTYLE	YOUR SCORE				
1.	Do you actively listen?	1	2	3	4	5
2.	Do you consider yourself a good role model?	1	2	3	4	5
3.	Do you remain flexible when necessary?	1	2	3	4	5
4.	Do you maintain a forgiving attitude?	1	2	3	4	5
5.	Do you prioritize building the self-esteem of others?	1	2	3	4	5
6.	How often do you express love and respect?	1	2	3	4	5
7.	How often do you have meals together?	1	2	3	4	5
8.	How are your family relationships?	1	2	3	4	5
9.	How well do you deal with conflict and disagreements?	1	2	3	4	5
10.	How often do you spend quality time together?	1	2	3	4	5
11.	How fulfilled do you feel in your family time?	1	2	3	4	5

Total: _____

Based on your score, what are the top four lifestyle changes you would like to work on this week? List those below.

FOR LIFESTYLE CHANGE IN
THE FAMILY SPOKE

GOAL 1	
GOAL 2	
GOAL 3	
GOAL 4	

What can you implement daily to increase this area of balance in your life? As you move through the week, consider the daily action items and how they relate to the four priority goals of improvement you have listed above. On the journal page, be sure to include the action items you have chosen and include your thoughts, fears, progress, etc.

The Most Important Meeting of the Week

"Again, truly I tell you that if two of you on earth agree about anything they ask for, it will be done for them by my Father in heaven."

—THE BIBLE

Today, I want to share my experience with the family *POWER Meeting*. Hopefully you have been holding these *POWER meetings* once a week for the past four weeks. Let me tell you why these are so important!

You may be wondering why I would want to have another meeting? But, in agreement with Mr. Ziglar, I believe this meeting can change your lives forever.

The format of our meeting has changed over the years, but the sweet spot of our family meeting for years was sandwiched between a time of worship on Saturday or Sunday and the start of the work week on Monday. For you, this sacred time could be on Sunday afternoon, or it could be another day of your work week that is different. It isn't the day that is the most important, but it is the consistency of the time to meet, both with yourself and with your people.

When our family implements this practice, we experience great benefits:

> We are aligned for the week.
> We are individually motivated to accomplish our personal goals.
> We have communicated and are connected and covered as a team.

These attributes produce greater goal achievement, peaceful family members, and proactively prevent miscommunication. They also help to connect us and heal any bitterness that might have built up since our last family meeting.

What does it take to make a great week, and what does it take to make a great family?

There are many factors we will discuss as we delve into it more this week. But for us, building a great family starts with a simple meeting on Sunday nights.

My dad, Sam Henning, conducted regular family meetings with our family. We also had devotions most mornings when I was growing up. I remember my grandfather, Earl Henning, doing these same family meetings and bible stories with us too. As a child, these were not always times I looked forward to because, well, you know how kids and teenagers are. I didn't see the importance and wanted to get on with my own life. I'm pretty sure my brother Justin didn't want to do them either! We would fight and were so annoyed that our parents made us get together.

But now as I'm looking back decades later on what a great dad I have, these meetings were some of our core gathering times and I remember them. I knew I would have to report on my activities and give an account of my goals. In fact, my dad let me set goals at these meetings. We made achievement charts, and we even got to earn prizes. I remember getting new roller skates and another time new Gloria Vanderbilt jeans when I reached some of my goals. These meetings were fun!!

Sometimes adjustments had to be made in the form of discipline and correction. At other times, we celebrated and were encouraged. The family meeting had a profound effect on me as a growing individual. I knew where I stood in life and with my parents. I knew my family believed in me. My parents were unified, and my brother and I were a part of family decisions. My dad made sure to "inspect what he expected" and to "criticize the performance, not the performer." My parents have one of the best marriages I've ever seen, and I firmly believe it's because they have connected for years at these family *POWER meetings*.

You may run a similar meeting in your home, either with yourself, if you are single, or with your family.

If you hold this most important meeting of the week, I believe your family will be blessed, your goals will be achieved, and you will see results like never before. If you haven't tried this yet, will you step outside of your comfort zone and do this? It will open your eyes to thoughts, concerns, goals, and successes you may have never seen before.

IDEAS FOR ACTION:

- Don't skimp on your meeting this week. Hold a meeting with yourself and hold a meeting with your family. Keep yourself accountable to your week ahead and to what you want to achieve.
- Make sure you are using a good calendar. If you haven't yet incorporated your yearly goals into quarterly goals, monthly goals, weekly goals, and bite-sized to-do lists, work on that today.

Go and be full of POWER!

P **P**rayer Requests
O **O**ld Business
W **W**hat's Next?
E **E**xpectations
R **R**oles, Responsibilities, and Resources

JOURNAL

Based on the Family Assessment and Ideas for Action,
what can you do today to improve your focus?

Remember:
Analyze (reflect deeply)
Activate (determine an action item)
Accelerate (utilize your resources and strengths)

What Kind of Role Model are You?

*"Your greatest contribution may not be something
you do, but someone you raise."*

—ANDY STANLEY

Because we are so close to our family members, it can be hard to give one another grace because we so often see one another in our weaknesses. We are familiar with one another through it all — the good, the bad and the ugly.

They know when we are tired.

They see our messes.

They know when we have bad attitudes.

These inconsistencies can result in our family members tuning us out pretty easily.

**You've heard it said, "More is caught than is taught,"
and as it relates to family, I firmly agree.**

A few years ago, I decided I wanted to be liked MOST by the people who knew me BEST. I had a lot of friends and maybe even some admirers, but more than anything, I wanted my kids to grow up liking me. And I wanted my husband to like me. And I want my parents to like me, and my brother too. I decided to stop giving my best away every time I walked out my door.

Most of us realize we have to be "on" when we leave our homes. In other words, we have to perform our best at work, at church, in social situations, at the gym, or even volunteering. But we have to remember we cannot spend our best energy "on" the world because when we arrive home, we will be "off" to the people who need us the most.

Your home should be your castle and your place of rest. But it should also be the best training ground for those closest to us. It should provide a haven of peace for your family and be a place of recreation, fun, education, growth, honesty and development.

We can't give away our best energy to our work, careers, the world, friends, those who need our counsel, etc. We have to keep reserves for those we love most.

IDEAS FOR ACTION:

- Are you reserving your best energy for your family? If not, how can you change the order of things around your home?

- Have you built enough trust with those in your home that they would ask you to mentor them or ask for your advice?

- What kind of role model are you? Do you model kindness, patience, and love? Do you go out of your way to ensure your family knows how much you care?

- What characteristics of a leader are you displaying in your home?

Whether you're a parent, an aunt, a sister, or a brother, whether you work full-time, part-time, or not at all, whether you are a great teacher, a giving servant, or both, it matters not. Remember, my friends, to be nicest to those who know you best. We only get one life, and our families will carry our legacy long after we are gone. Let's be sure to invest in them the most!

JOURNAL

Based on the Family Assessment and Ideas for Action,
what can you do today to improve your focus?

Remember:
Analyze (reflect deeply)
Activate (determine an action item)
Accelerate (utilize your resources and strengths)

Strong Roots

"The days go slow, and the years go fast."

−EVERY PARENT EVER

Building a great family isn't always easy because we don't see progress every day. When you are single, building your family is limitless because you can spend time with people from all walks of life in different settings. When you are married, your spouse is your family. When you add children, your family increases. No matter what your family looks like, these principles apply in helping you build and maintain strong roots.

This reminds me of the story of the Chinese Bamboo Tree:

> When this particular seed is planted, watered, and nurtured for years, it doesn't grow upward as much as an inch. Nothing happens for the first year. There's no sign of growth. Not even a hint. The same thing happens or doesn't happen in the second year. And then the third year.
>
> The tree is carefully watered and fertilized each year, but nothing shows. No growth. No anything. And so it goes as the sun rises

and sets for four solid years. The farmer and his wife have nothing tangible to show for this labor or effort.

Then, along comes year five. After five years of fertilizing and watering have passed, with nothing to show for it, the bamboo tree suddenly sprouts and grows eighty feet in just six weeks!

Does the little tree lie dormant for four years only to grow exponentially in the fifth? Or was the little tree growing underground, developing a strong root system to support its potential for outward growth in the fifth year and beyond? The answer is, of course, obvious. Had the tree not developed a strong unseen foundation, it could not have sustained its life as it grew."

This story applies to many aspects of our lives: growing a business, becoming a successful individual, raising a great family, and so much more. There are many years when our toil is unseen. Yes, our kids may be growing little by little, and we may also notice changes in our own growth. But as a family, it can sometimes seem like forever until we see the tiniest piece of fruit on what we have planted.

And yet it is with great intention that we set family goals, continue to plant, day after day, into our marriages, our relationships, our children, our grandchildren, our parents, our siblings, our friends, and our extended families. Each day we plant into our legacy.

So, how do we build a great family? Maybe it's just that we do the great things needed every day:

We show love.
We listen.
We serve.
We teach, explain and model.
We remain principled yet flexible.

We build the security of others.

We forgive.

We express our gratitude.

We have meals together.

We show honor and respect.

We deal with disagreements and conflict in a healthy and mature way.

We invest time together.

We do what other family members need, even when it is inconvenient for us.

I thought of this one day as I drove our son Ethan to piano lessons, which were the hardest appointment to get to each week. We drove 40 minutes in peak rush-hour traffic to get there. I usually picked up some of our other kids at the same time and had someone doing homework in the back seat. And I'm usually tired by this hour.

But as soon as we entered the door of the piano teacher, I knew it was worth it. The traffic. The crying of my children. The cooking ahead. The organizing schedules. The drive. I knew this little hour was a sacred moment in our day. A moment for our young son to learn a skill that was important in his development. It's also a moment for me to take in the music and just sit and rest. Why I had to drive so far for this experience, I'm not quite sure. But I'm assured this little thing, this act of love, this driving and doing and loving and serving, is an incredible investment in our son.

This is what my parents did for me.

This is what it takes to build a great family. Now that we have three amazing grown sons, each over 6 feet tall, I can say it again, but with so much perspective! The days are long, but the years are so fast. Soon, you too will see your little bamboo trees shoot up into all you thought they could be!

- Look at the list for building a great family. How are you doing? In what areas can you improve?

- Be encouraged. Even though you can't see it now, growth is taking place underground. Just wait. Your family, your spouse, and your legacy are on their way.

- Stay dedicated to your family goals and the habits that you are building daily.

JOURNAL

Based on the Family Assessment and Ideas for Action,
what can you do today to improve your focus?

Remember:
Analyze (reflect deeply)
Activate (determine an action item)
Accelerate (utilize your resources and strengths)

It Starts with Manners

"Please and thank you are still magic words."

–MOM

I'm thankful for my mother-in-law, Toni Hellwig. She's the dearest of Southern ladies, born in Baltimore, but raised mostly in Dillon, South Carolina and now living in Georgia. Miss Toni is one of the kindest and most grateful people I know. My husband calls her a saint, and I think she's one too! My family today wouldn't be what it is without her consistent and insistent teaching of this timeless principle.

Although her family was broken by divorce (her mom raised five children as a single parent in the 1950s and 60s in the south), and they didn't have much by the world's standards, her mother (Miss Clara) insisted upon the use of "Yes, ma'am," "Please" and "Thank You." And Miss Toni ensured her own four children grew up minding their manners. Now my husband, Jay, demands the same from our children, and I am grateful.

My mother-in-law has helped teach me what it means to grow a great family. It's about being grateful, and it starts with minding our manners.

I recently read an article by Mark King entitled, "The Decline of Manners in America." The article quotes a UCLA study highlighting the "stark drop in the use of the word 'please' among adults, with only 7% of individuals using it in requests." The study and article go on to say, "The word 'please' is "increasingly employed as a tool to exert pressure on others to comply with requests, rather than as a genuine expression of politeness." Rude driving behaviors, an increased use of profanity, lack of appreciation for service workers, government officials and even our own family members have led to an increasingly hostile society. Social Media has also amplified incivility. While people are behind their screens, they feel free to engage in insults, name-calling, personal attacks and even threats. According to the article, "This has created a pervasive environment of disrespect and incivility online, where basic courtesy is often abandoned in favor of hostile and inflammatory behavior. The ripple effects of online rudeness extend beyond the digital world, influencing how people interact in real life."

Wow! What is our world becoming and how can we help?

I am reminded by a study Mr. Ziglar often quoted. "Psychiatrist Smiley Blanton says that roughly 80% of all the counseling he does is the direct result of parents not having taught their children manners."

To build a great family, let's start with teaching manners. We must prioritize basic manners such as please and thank you and extend our teaching to humility, kindness and following the golden rule, "Do unto others as you would have them do unto you."

And let's also remember to practice our manners with our family members. Sometimes it seems we are the rudest to those closest to us. We can't get too comfortable, too complacent or become too rushed or busy to neglect this cause.

Let's reach our goals and be courteous as we do so.

- How are your manners? We may not even realize when we forget to say please, thank you, be cordial and courteous with our family members, and have an attitude of honor.

- Encourage your children and grandchildren to follow the golden rule. Post it up in your home and quote it often until it is ingrained in them and practiced. Your tireless efforts will not go unrewarded.

> If we mind our manners, I think we could change the world! We never know how a simple "thank you" might impact generations to come.

JOURNAL

Based on the Family Assessment and Ideas for Action,
what can you do today to improve focus?

Remember:
Analyze (reflect deeply)
Activate (determine an action item)
Accelerate (utilize your resources and strengths)

What's the Missing Ingredient?

"No person was ever honored for what he received.
Honor has been the reward for what he gave."

−CALVIN COOLIDGE

When my kids were growing up, they loved watching cooking shows. Their favorite was a show where four up-and-coming chefs competed at turning everyday items into an extraordinary three-course meal before a panel of expert judges. Course by course, the chefs were eliminated from the competition until only one winner remained.

Despite the fact that their mother is not a very good cook (or maybe *because* she is not a cook at all), my kids loved seeing how the ingredients the chefs chose would weave themselves into perfect dishes.

Inevitably, one of the chefs would overlook a key ingredient or completely forget it. This made me wonder if there is one key ingredient *we* have been missing in families and in relationships altogether. If so, are our families and relationships being eliminated because we don't know what it is?

I want to propose that one key ingredient many of us are missing is HONOR.

HONOR VS. RESPECT

In his book, *Winology: 9 Steps to Winning in Life, Business and Relationships*, my friend Joel Scrivner, six-time national and four-time world champion martial artist turned pastor / author / speaker, discusses the "universal force" of honor.

> "One of the fundamental martial arts training requirements is to treat those who are your seniors in a certain manner. And this honor is not rooted in the other person's conduct or behavior but rather in their position and title. While respect is based on conduct and behavior and must be earned, honor is a positional entity that has an incredibly symbiotic empowering quality. When you give honor, you receive honor." [5]

To sum it up, respect is conditional, honor is positional, and investing in honor absolutely works.

WHERE'S OUR HONOR?

Have we lost this quality, this key ingredient in our American culture? Do we still treat our senior citizens with the esteem they deserve?

Do we revere our bosses, our elders, our mothers and fathers, our leaders, our teachers, police officers, civic workers, our military and our elected officials simply because of the position they hold? Or are we waiting to do so until they "earn our respect"?

In a world where we are all free to give our opinions, to make our voices heard, to "be who we want to be," in this culture of individualization, have we forgotten what the people who came before us did to help us get to where we are?

What does a family that practices honor look like?

I believe they:

Listen to those who have helped them and gone before them.

Give deference to the voice of their elders.

Practice self-sacrifice in order to care for their parents and grandparents.

Admire the character of older siblings who have gone before them.

Practice honor in both directions, from younger to older and older to younger.

Respect and seek harmony among the generations.

No longer have to start from scratch, with each new generation paving a way of its own.

Instead, children receive a ready inheritance from their parents because they receive and accept wisdom and knowledge.

These are just a few of the benefits we can consider. Investing in honor is sure to yield a great return. Order is found in our homes, marriages, families, communities, and nations when we choose honor.

Let's find this ingredient again. Maybe it's just shoved in the back of our pantry and needs to be rediscovered. Let's find our honor.

IDEAS FOR ACTION:

- Revere and esteem someone tomorrow just because of their position, even when it is hard.

- Think about how your family honors each other in relationship. Is there room for improvement? Have a family meeting and discuss what steps you will take to honor one another more.

- Remember this—you don't have to start from scratch. Honor those who've gone before you and accelerate your advancement. Start putting this reverence into practice yourself and your children will follow.

JOURNAL

Based on the Family Assessment and Ideas for Action,
what can you do today to improve your focus?

Remember:
Analyze (reflect deeply)
Activate (determine an action item)
Accelerate (utilize your resources and strengths)

A Little of This Can Go a Long Way

"Levity is that pull that lifts us above our problems, above our weakness, above our failures, and above our fears."

–JILL HELLWIG

There are many resources to help make a family great. When it comes to achieving our goals as a family, all of us, from our spouses, parents, siblings, and kids, need to have FUN together too.

Remember, life isn't ALL about work.

What makes a family fun?

While that is different for us all, there is one uncommon word that brings a bit of joy to life – levity. My mentor Bryan Flanagan often reminded me of this when I was too stuck in my career goals and not having enough fun. He used to tell me, *"Jill, angels fly because they take themselves lightly."*

I'm sure Bryan told me this because I tend to get hyper-focused on my goals and forget about the fun part. Although I love to laugh, I do not consider myself humorous or funny. When I tell you this is something I've had to work at, I am serious.

One time I was hanging out with a new group of girlfriends. While I was very close to one of the girls in the group, she was the one close to the other girls. And this group was hilarious. One joke after the other, they would banter back and forth with quick wit I only wished I had. In fact, I wished I had it so badly that when I went home from being with that group that night, I went home and googled "how to be funny." Yes, I did that. Always the student, I googled "how to be funny." Now, I think THAT is funny! When I tell people that story, they laugh and laugh, and I laugh at myself. And laughing at those idiosyncrasies in us all is what makes us fun.

Levity adds lightness to our goals. Life can be weighty, heavy, and hard. Why have all these goals if we can't add a bit of fun to our days as well? We can't take ourselves so seriously all the time.

According to the 1838 Miriam-Webster Dictionary,

> "Levity originally was thought to be a physical force exactly like gravity but pulling in the opposite direction, like the helium in a balloon. As recently as the 19th century, scientists were still arguing about its existence. Today's *levity* refers only to lightness in manner. To stern believers of some religious faiths, levity is often regarded as almost sinful. But the word, like its synonym *frivolity*, now has an old-fashioned ring to it and is usually used only half-seriously."

My husband is great at this. He works very hard but finds things to laugh at throughout each day. Whether it is people watching or funny videos, or whether we're going to see a comedian live or watch videos on Netflix, he is the fun to my serious, and I so appreciate it.

The Bible says, *"A merry heart is good medicine!"* and Mr. Ziglar used to say it like this, "It's bad to suppress laughter. If you do, it goes back down and spreads your hips!" Well, I'm not getting fat, and I am staying merry and young.... even if I have to google how to be funny.

What about you?
What do you do to add a bit of levity to your days?

I think we can take a few tips from our kids and other children in our lives.

ITEMS FOR ACTION:

- Let's laugh, play, jump, sing, tell jokes, tickle and run around in circles!
- Let's take ourselves lightly and chuckle at our silly mistakes.
- Let's be a fun family this week.
- Allow the energy of levity to make your family SOAR!

JOURNAL

Based on the Family Assessment and Ideas for Action,
what can you do today to improve your focus?

Remember:
Analyze (reflect deeply)
Activate (determine an action item)
Accelerate (utilize your resources and strengths)

A Greater Family, Both Gathered and On the Go

"The church is not an organization you join;
it is a family where you belong."

−NICKY GUMBEL

Today is our last day to talk about family. I would be remiss if I did not discuss one of the greatest families you have at your disposal: the CHURCH.

Yes, I know the church is a complex topic. We all come from different backgrounds, denominations, faiths, and experiences. Some of us have been hurt by the church, and some of us have been found in church. No matter where you are at this season in life, I want to encourage you to keep reading.

My grandparents, Earl and Joyce Henning were church planters and pastors for over 50 years. My parents, Sam and Judy Henning, were pastors for over 50 years and my husband and I are ordained pastors. I'm a church girl. I have been seated on the pews almost my entire life. I often say if I had a nickel for every church service I've attended, I'd own an island!

While I love the church, I have also experienced hurt by the people in the church, sometimes the leaders, and sometimes well-meaning people who have criticized our family's leadership. There has been room for wounding for which I've had to be healed. But I have had a profound relationship with the church, and I still believe it is for today.

You might ask how this relates to setting goals. I believe this element is so integral to our fulfillment in life that I want to give it special emphasis. If you would allow it or allow it again,

The Church can be your family. When it is authentic, and relationships are developed and tested over time, I believe you can be enriched by a church family as much or even more than by your blood relatives.

> *"While Jesus was still talking to the crowd, his mother and brothers stood outside, wanting to speak to him. Someone told him, 'Your mother and brothers are standing outside, wanting to speak to you.'*
>
> *"He replied to him, 'Who is my mother, and who are my brothers?' Pointing to his disciples, he said, 'Here are my mother and my brothers. For whoever does the will of my Father in heaven is my brother and sister and mother.'"*
>
> Mark 3:31-35

I believe Jesus makes it clear in this passage that we can have family in the context of discipleship.

The Church is so much bigger than a group of people attending worship services for a one and a half hour long meeting each week. One role of The Church is to come together so we can gather and be refreshed. Further, after we are charged up, equipped, and taught, we must go into the world and BE the church. In other words, we must become on the go throughout the week so we can bring more people into our family for a chance at real love and fellowship.

Many no longer come to church each Sunday. Prior to the pandemic of 2020, according to *Pew* magazine, the statistics for church attendance were in decline, with the most significant number of members no longer attending in the millennial generation. Of course, during the pandemic of 2020, many churches were shut down and even closed for good. People could not attend services for many weeks and many people have never returned. This disruption has impacted all generations.

So, we've got a complex issue that needs to be addressed.

> Why are our family members leaving the church?
> Is there hope for future generations?

If this is you, I hurt with you.

The Church must provide a loving family relationship that is coupled with humble Christian discipleship every single day of the week.

People talk about Christians who are hypocrites. They see supposed Christians who attend church making mistakes and not living out their faith at work, at school, on the field or in their actions toward others. We have seen many scandals in the church in recent years as well, causing a lack of faith, trust and confidence in the integrity of our church pastors and leaders.

While it makes sense that people would be turned off by the church because of inauthentic and even unethical people, it's important for us to recognize that Christians aren't perfect people. They have never been, and they never will be, just like families aren't perfect. I am not gving grace here to abusive and toxic situations. It is important for the church to be holy and righteous and not be a place of hurt for the sheep of our flocks. Sin is real. Sin is missing the mark and not living up to the standards as outlined in the word of God. We've got to teach the next generations the importance of consecrating ourselves to God and His word, while not looking to humans to be sinless. We must each take responsibility for our own faith by looking to the Word of God as our guide. Yes, we're inadequate, we're not perfect, and we fail time and time again, and yet we must also be committed to becoming disciples of our faith.

I believe the benefits of Christian fellowship are many: deep relationships, a place to belong, a place to serve, give and grow your gifts and talents. That's what church is to me and what church can be when we commit and give it a chance like it's our family. Church and church people will always disappoint us, but through forgiveness, humility, communication, and love, we can work together to change our world.

Let's go be the church gathered, and also the church on the GO, so we can make an impact and realize our goals.

IDEAS FOR ACTION:

- Today is accountability day! Share with your accountability partner the steps you made toward your set goals this past week.

- Take notice of bad habits you need to replace with good ones. What one bad habit can you replace next week?

- Find one new encouraging voice to listen to and add that to your schedule.

- Have you set aside time each week to gather with fellow believers to be discipled and refreshed? (Hint: this one act alone can help you in goal achievement because your deepest, most profound relationships can come in the context of loving support through your Christian friends.)

- Have you set yourself on mission each day as an ambassador for the church while you GO about your daily duties? To whom are you representing in your daily field? Is it Christ first?

- Are you living an authentic Christian life that compels others to want what you have?

- Would your children want to stay a part of the Christian faith because of your daily walk?

I don't want us to lose even one of our family members, and that includes you.

If you've been hurt, offended, or disillusioned by the church, I acknowledge your wounds and offer a prayer for healing so you can walk out all you are called to do on this earth. When we find our family in church, we find and fulfill our created purpose in Christ.

Let's GO be the church!
Let's GO build a family!

Prayer:

Dear Father,

Thank you for the Church. I pray that everyone reading this prayer will be healed of any wounds inflicted by a Christian or by an act of a church member or leader. God, when we come together and worship you, there is ignited faith in our assembly and power in our agreement. We are learning from your Word and taking this teaching to others who so desperately need you. While the pandemic might have kept us from entering a church building for many months, I thank you that we are meeting again. I pray that a new, fresh wind of your Holy Spirit will ignite a generation to follow you like never before. I pray that our churches and church leaders will be full of righteousness so that they can be used as vessels of honor for your glory. I pray that the church will rise to minister to all who have a need, to the orphans and the widows, to those naked, alone, imprisoned, hungry and thirsty. I pray that anyone reading this prayer will be comforted to know the church is alive and well and you are returning for a bride without a spot or wrinkle. Lord, I pray that we will find family in the church. Allow for authentic relationships that produce disciples for you. I pray each person will feel loved and accepted and have a place with other disciples where they can run after you together. Help those reading this prayer find just the right church for them and their family. Illuminate this body of believers and help them to connect in a lasting, real and significant way.

In Jesus' name,
Amen

JOURNAL

Based on the Family Assessment and Ideas for Action,
what can you do today to improve your focus?

Remember:
Analyze (reflect deeply)
Activate (determine an action item)
Accelerate (utilize your resources and strengths)

WEEK SIX

Financial Wholeness

GETTING INTO THE MINDSET OF MANAGING OUR FINANCES WITH INTEGRITY AND WISDOM

The first assignment for this week is to hold the most important meeting of the week: the *POWER meeting,* so you can determine the priorities and scheduling for the week. While it is different for everyone, and circumstances change from week to week, there are a few components to the weekly meeting that are necessary for success:

- Bring your calendar.
- Bring your current goals and needs for the coming week.
- Commit your week to each other and to God.

THE MOST IMPORTANT MEETING OF THE WEEK

WEEK OF ....

P PRAYER
REQUEST

O OLD
BUSINESS

W WHAT'S
NEXT?

E EXPECTATIONS

R ROLES,
RESPONSIBILITIES,
AND RESOURCES

"The place of agreement is the place of power." Matthew 18:19

NIGHTLY BRAIN RELEASE - JOURNALING

My thoughts, ideas, concerns and worries

- [ ] ....
- [ ] ....
- [ ] ....
- [ ] ....
- [ ] ....
- [ ] ....
- [ ] ....
- [ ] ....
- [ ] ....
- [ ] ....

What is God saying about these items?

- [ ] ....
- [ ] ....
- [ ] ....
- [ ] ....
- [ ] ....
- [ ] ....

PRODUCTIVITY SCHEDULE

WEEK OF:

SUNDAY

G Y R
G Y R
G Y R
G Y R

MONDAY

G Y R
G Y R
G Y R
G Y R

TUESDAY

G Y R
G Y R
G Y R
G Y R

WEDNESDAY

G Y R
G Y R
G Y R
G Y R

THURSDAY

G Y R
G Y R
G Y R
G Y R

FRIDAY

G Y R
G Y R
G Y R
G Y R

SATURDAY

G Y R
G Y R
G Y R
G Y R

MY TOP 4 PRIORITY GOALS

○ _____
○ _____
○ _____
○ _____

THIS WEEK'S TOP THREE PRIORITIES, PROJECTS & PEOPLE

○ _____
○ _____
○ _____

IMPORTANT NOTES

Weekly Focus

FINANCIAL SPOKE

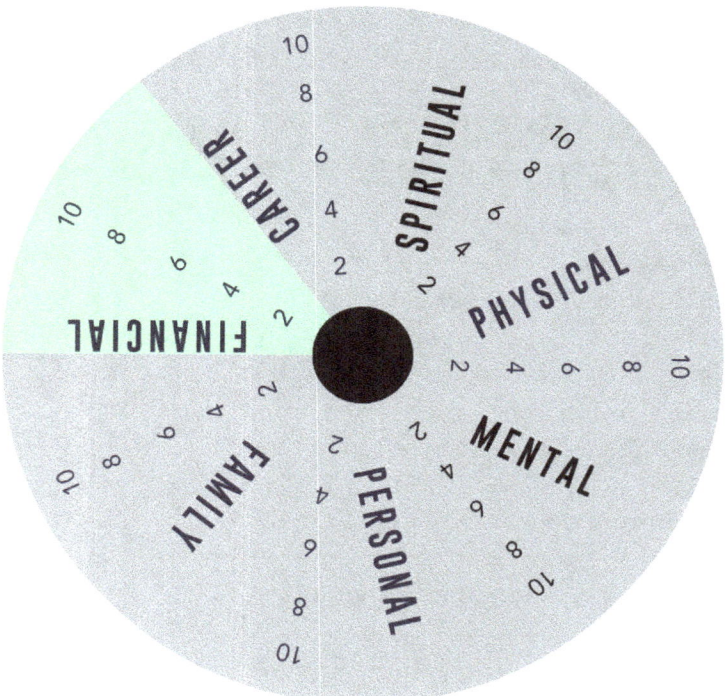

The issue of finances can bring a lot of stress into the lives of individuals and families. It's such an important issue; the Bible mentions money over 800 times and makes over 2,000 financial references. These numbers show us the importance of managing our finances with integrity and wisdom. The Bible also alerts us to the fact that money can pull us in unhealthy directions if we don't understand it is our role to manage it and not allow it to manage us.

On the next page is an assessment of the Financial Spoke on the Wheel of Life. Take your time and consider each question. Circle the answer that best reflects your current lifestyle.

Wheel of Life

FINANCIAL ASSESSMENT

Circle the answer that best reflects your current lifestyle.
Take the time to reflect on these.

YOUR CURRENT LIFESTYLE	YOUR SCORE
1. Are your finances a priority?	1 2 3 4 5
2. Do you stick to your personal budget?	1 2 3 4 5
3. How often do you make impulse purchases?	1 2 3 4 5
4. How satisfied are you with your income?	1 2 3 4 5
5. Are you currently living within your means?	1 2 3 4 5
6. How often are you able to put money into savings?	1 2 3 4 5
7. Do you have adequate insurance?	1 2 3 4 5
8. Are you able to invest in the projects you would like?	1 2 3 4 5
9. How aware are you of your financial statements?	1 2 3 4 5
10. Are you living debt free?	1 2 3 4 5
11. Do you give generously and pursue your dreams?	1 2 3 4 5

Total: _____

Based on your score, what are the top four lifestyle changes you would like to work on this week? List those below.

FOR LIFESTYLE CHANGE IN
THE FINANCIAL SPOKE

GOAL 1	
GOAL 2	
GOAL 3	
GOAL 4	

What can you implement daily to increase this area of balance in your life? As you move through the week, consider the daily action items and how they relate to the four priority goals of improvement you have listed above. On the journal page, be sure to include the action items you have chosen and include your thoughts, fears, progress, etc.

DAY 36

May You Prosper

*"I hope that you enjoy good health and
that all may go well with you,
even as your soul is getting along well! And I hope that you
prosper even as your soul prospers!"*

–THE BIBLE

May you prosper!

As you follow your purpose, calling, and assignment, I hope you will be rewarded richly with prosperity. It is okay, and it is part of a good plan for us to prosper.

To prosper means that we are thriving and doing well financially. In order to do what we are called to do, we need resources. Yet, it's important to note that money isn't first. In fact, I included it last in our lessons because money should not be our primary focus. When we get the rest of our life in alignment, prosperity should naturally follow.

Money does not grow on trees, but doors of opportunity will open for us as our priorities are aligned with our purpose.

Finances aren't everything, but they play a significant role in our overall life satisfaction. As Mr. Ziglar used to say,

> "Money isn't everything, but it is reasonably close to oxygen."
>
> and
>
> "I've had it and I haven't had it, and I can tell you, it's better to have it."

I want to give you encouragement and, for some of you, the needed permission to desire prosperity as you align all your goals.

As you do the right things every day, following through on what you have learned on this journey, I believe you will be in good health and prosper, even as your very soul prospers.

IDEAS FOR ACTION:

- Think about the word "prosperity." What does it mean to you and what connotation does it have?
- Do you need to change your money mindsets and give yourself permission to prosper?
- How do you think following through on the other priorities on the various spokes of the wheel will help you to prosper?
- Be encouraged. Your goals are closer than you think. Keep Going!
- Is money your primary goal? Consider putting your purpose first and then the money will follow.

JOURNAL

Based on the Financial Assessment and Ideas for Action,
what can you do today to improve your focus?

Remember:
Analyze (reflect deeply)
Activate (determine an action item)
Accelerate (utilize your resources and strengths)

Scarcity or Generosity? Which do you Believe?

Let's declare this out loud:
"Scarcity: Be gone! Generosity: Make your home in my heart!"

Our personal finances can reflect our belief system.

A few years ago, I wrote a heartfelt prayer. I asked God to take out all the lack in my life and replace it with grace. I'm not sure why I penned those exact words, except that I was "spent" and running on empty. I felt scarcity everywhere, and my perspective needed a shift.

What's our attitude about our resources?

While America is the most generous nation in the world (we give the most), I wonder if we could be even more generous if our attitudes did not also reflect scarcity.

The definition of scarcity: (*n*) the state of being scarce or in short supply; shortage. "A time of scarcity."

While this definition is helpful, let's go a step further. I'm no economist, but I'm going to give this topic a whirl.

It's an economic principle.

In the 1970s, there was a gasoline shortage in America. I still remember waiting as a young child in the car with my parents, lined up for miles to get to the gas pumps in Houston, TX. I remember the endless cars waiting. I still see in my memory, Texans, red gasoline containers in hand, hoping to not only fill their tanks for that trip but to fill their containers for the future. Supply was low, demand was high, and gasoline was scarce.

I wonder if too many of us are walking around each day like there is a shortage of our own resources. Are our wants more than what we believe about our supply? Are we carrying around our own little red gas cans, trying to keep all we can, afraid to give too much away, and worried there won't be enough? Are we self-preserving and protecting ourselves just in case tomorrow doesn't hold what we need?

Do we need to temper the wants in our lives?

Maybe you can identify with this feeling regarding your personal finances. When the debts are high and the bills are high, we can begin to think there is not enough. We look at our balance sheets and they aren't adding up. What we think we need is in short supply as our month is more than our money.

Some of us may not have a lack in our finances, but maybe we feel a shortage in another area—time or help or wisdom or friendship. No matter the resource, we feel there are insufficient funds to give us what we need. Our wants are greater than our provision.

What if we shifted our attitudes? Instead of focusing on our wants and believing our bank account is too low, our income is not enough, or our provision is not great, what if we focused our efforts on what we *do* have?

While a scarcity mindset is defeating and diminishing, a lifestyle of grace is empowering.

- Meditate on gratitude and be thankful for an abundant supply in your life.

- Live with grace by being empowered with what you do have.

- There will come a time when we have shortages in our world again. How can you be prepared with a storehouse, as Joseph prepared Egypt in Genesis?

JOURNAL

Based on the Financial Assessment and Ideas for Action,
what can you do today to improve your focus?

Remember:
Analyze (reflect deeply)
Activate (determine an action item)
Accelerate (utilize your resources and strengths)

The Great Flip

"By flipping your perspective, you can flip your results."

−JILL HELLWIG

This is a continuation from Day 37, Scarcity or Generosity? Which do you Believe?

What if we did the great flip? Or you could call it looking at the other side of the coin.

> Rather than allowing the lack in our life to occupy all our mental space and energy, what if we focused instead on the grace given us for this moment?
>
> What if our flip involved letting go of those things we hold so tightly, releasing what little we think we have to a plan that's bigger than we could imagine?
>
> What if we took this a step further—not only focusing on our good supply but shifting our scarcity mindset to a generosity quotient?

While being grateful that what we have is more than enough (no scarcity), we also should focus on extending a helping hand to those in need. We choose to look for ways to be generous and to teach our children to do so. We look for opportunities to bless others. And we fully expect in this process to have our own needs met.

Do you think flipping the coin could change our lives?

My main objective is to help you to see this: when you start to feel lack, as we sometimes will, remember to be grateful and generous instead. I firmly believe that when we do the great flip, relying on grace instead of focusing on our wants and demands, we will have more to be grateful for, and we will again become the most generous nation in the world—both in our hearts and in our pocketbooks.

Let's agree to have so much that we won't know where to give it all. It's possible and probable when we shift our beliefs.

IDEAS FOR ACTION:

- Shift your level of wants so your supply can be greater.
- Move from consumer to giver.
- Reread this again and again as you digest this information and change your perspective.

JOURNAL

Based on the Financial Assessment and Ideas for Action,
what can you do today to improve your focus?

Remember:
Analyze (reflect deeply)
Activate (determine an action item)
Accelerate (utilize your resources and strengths)

Find Your Flow

"Flow is a verb, meaning to proceed smoothly and readily, or to have a smooth continuity."

—MIRIAM WEBSTER

Have you heard the saying, "Find Your Flow"?

Sometimes it is easier for us to simply ask someone to replicate or duplicate exactly what we are doing. We can teach our kids, employees, and those around us to "do as we do." This is the easier way, but if we go this route, all we are doing is creating replicas of ourselves instead of authentic human beings who can transfer the concepts we've taught into easily adaptable principles within their own gifts and strengths.

With every concept I teach, I hope the principles themselves will guide you and you can adapt them for your best use. I hope you can implement these teachings into your life flow, workflow, and creative zone. To me, this is helping my clients find their flow.

What is flow?

According to Wikipedia, "In positive psychology, flow, also known as the zone, is the mental state of operation in which a person performing an activity is fully immersed in a feeling of energized focus, full involvement, and enjoyment in the process of the activity. In essence, flow is characterized by complete absorption in what one does.

"Named by Mihály Csíkszentmihályi, achieving flow is often colloquially referred to as being in the zone."

As it relates to your goals and your business, flow is that sweet spot that gives you momentum, hyper-focus, and exceptional success.

I desire for your life to flow just as a river flows—continuously, steadily, and also readily and beautifully. When we "find our flow," we are bringing in resources continuously, speedily, and in abundance. And we are enjoying doing it because we are in the sweet spot of our happy zone.

So how do we best find our flow?

As it relates to our financial goals, we have to be a source of continuous generosity. When we give, we release the supernatural flow of abundance into the earth. No longer does our money stay stagnant in a bank account or an investment somewhere, but it is released into the hands of someone else so it can be used for the greater good. When we release our flow to others, the gift of abundance will surely come back to us. Instead of being bottled up or stagnant, we become a continuous flow of enrichment for others.

IDEAS FOR ACTION:

- What one thing can you do today to help you find your flow?
- In what ways can you be more generous so your life is a continual flow of blessings?

JOURNAL

Based on the Financial Assessment and Ideas for Action,
what can you do today to improve your foucs?

Remember:
Analyze (reflect deeply)
Activate (determine an action item)
Accelerate (utilize your resources and strengths)

Is This the End?

"Just when the caterpillar thought her
life was over, she began to fly."

A PROVERB

It may seem we've come to the end. After all, it's the last day of our 40-day transformation journey. I am so proud of you, but this is ONLY THE BEGINNING!

What goals have you achieved in the last 40 days?
What mindsets have been shifted?
What thought processes have been impacted?
What has been STARTED in you?

My desire is that your life will continue to be made brand new. May you never again start a new year, or a new month, or a new day, without a clear focus on the goals you want to achieve and the motivation to inspire them to action.

I have gone along this 40-day journey just like you, and some days were not easy. But it is in the pressing where we know we are making progress. When we experience opposition, we should know we are doing something right.

Even if you do not think you have made the progress you expected, just remember you are still in the middle of the process. The words *process* and *progress* are just separated by 2 little letters; you are closer than you think!

You are being made new.
A Brand New You!

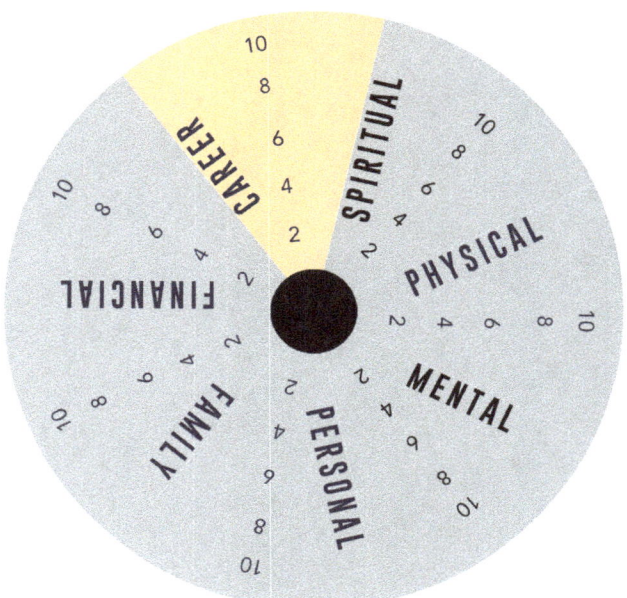

There is one more spoke of the Wheel of Life we have yet to cover. The Career Spoke. When all the other spokes come together, your career will too! As you continue to pursue excellence in the other priorities of life, I encourage you to get the skillset you need to excel in your career.

If this explanation frustrates you or if you feel this is too far out of your comfort zone to pursue on your own, I would love to help with this part of your journey.

Please consider registering for one of our ongoing classes. The course entitled *Brand New U* covers the areas of branding yourself for advancement in your business and/or career. The course entitled *Sell like a Girl* covers salesmanship – after all, we are all in sales. It is helpful in both your personal and professional life.

Either one of these experiences will help you advance in your career. You can find out more about these courses at my website, www.brandnewu.org.

Your Next Steps

Register for additional resources through my website, www.brandnewu.org.

If you would like to take your intensity up a notch, consider one-on-one coaching. This is where we see the greatest results. For more information, visit my website, www.brandnewu.org.

Invite me to speak to your group, organization, or company. Together, we will go deeper into the specific gaps you would like to see improved for your family, friends, church, and your entire team.

Epilogue

"But godliness with contentment is great gain."

—THE BIBLE

I was never that great at math, so maybe that is why implementing this little formula has taken me a bit more time than others. For most of my life, I have heard this scripture, but I'm not sure I understood it or applied it to my life until now.

Contentment is a hard concept for me. I love improving myself. I love setting goals. I love working toward my dreams. All my life, my parents taught me that "the sky's the limit," "you can make it happen," and "if it is to be, it's up to me"! These were the adages that have stuck with me into adulthood. So much so that I worked for a company known worldwide for improving the personal performance of millions and whose slogan is "it's about being better."

With these messages in mind, it has always been hard to grasp contentment. How can I be content when there is so much more I have to achieve? How can I be satisfied where I am when I have to get better, improve myself, and help someone else do the same?

What is contentment, anyway? Is it a state in life that anyone successful can ever achieve? But it hit me … contentment is a decision. It is a state of mind; godliness isn't enough if I want to get to a new level and see great gains. Sure, God loves when we are righteous and holy. But His Word clearly states that if we want great gains, the word contentment must come into play.

How can I explain how I realized this? I started understanding God's definition of contentment. True contentment comes from a total reliance on Him. Being content doesn't mean we have to be complacent, but it does say that instead of me doing more, only God can do more. Contentment doesn't ask, "Is this all there is?" Contentment says, "I am so grateful for what I have." With contentment, one wakes with peace, not feeling behind. Does that make sense? It has so moved me! I can now awake, and my first thought is, "I love my life. Thank you so very much, Lord." Instead of "What do I have to do today?" or "What do I need to improve to get where I want to go?"

However, I have found one secret to this concept of contentment. Maybe this is magic instead of science. The most interesting thing about it is that it requires great discipline – the discipline to make it a point to be content every day. It is the decision every morning to be grateful instead of being in pursuit. It is the daily decision to eat my provided manna instead of asking for meat.

The children of Israel seemed to have a similar dilemma to mine. In Numbers, chapter 11, they grumbled and whined to the Lord so much about their daily provision (manna), that He finally sent them so much meat that they got sick of it. I think we like to separate ourselves from those lost children of Israel, but how often have I whined to God about my provision, circumstance, and station in life? I am sure He has been a bit exasperated with me at times ... so much so that maybe He has even given me what I've asked for. But that meat isn't what is going to nourish me. It is only a substitution for the best nutrition He gives – the nourishment of the soul.

According to author Mike Cleveland,

> "It is especially important for us to note, too, that the manna given the Israelites was a picture representation of Jesus Christ. Jesus, like that manna, was given to us as nourishment for our souls. He is the living bread that came down from heaven to give His life for

all who would believe. Jesus said, *'I am the bread of life. Your fathers ate the manna in the wilderness, and they died. This is the bread that comes down out of heaven so that one may eat of it and not die. I am the living bread that came down out of heaven; if anyone eats of this bread, he will live forever; and the bread also which I will give for the life of the world is my flesh.'* (John 6:48-51)

"Those Israelites rejected the manna, which was given to them as a picture or type of Jesus Christ. Their rejection of the manna had a deeper significance than just wanting a change in diet. Their heart of discontentment was evidence that they were rejecting God Himself, preferring to gratify their fleshly cravings than feed contentedly on God's provision for them." [6]

I do not want to satisfy my flesh more than I want God's best for me. This laying down process is not easy. It requires sacrifice. However, the greatest sacrifice was made by our savior, Jesus Christ. He has given us the hope that we can be content and the grace (empowerment) to do so.

Finally, let's get to the best part – the great gains! With this equation, we get the best results of all – those God has for us. And then we are thankful wherever we are. I am amazed to see the great gains He has given me because of my new perspective. It is as though, suddenly, the things I've wished for are coming true: the promotions at work, the increase in prosperity, bad habits decreasing, beauty showing through, a growing marriage … and I am truly making great gains.

Let me say, however, it is not as though everything is perfect. I still have dreams and goals. The big difference is that I am content regardless of whether they happen because Jesus fulfills me every day. My focus is on Him, not where I need to go or what I need to do – just on who He is and all He's done for me. Now that perspective is what I call the greatest gain of all.

Maybe now that I'm content with whatever my circumstance, He knows He can trust me and give me more. And what's so neat about the "more" and the "great gains" is they are not just for me, but so I can help others know fulfillment.

All in all, I've decided that the power in this principle is not just in addition. I guess it is more similar to the multiplication process. As we start multiplying bigger and bigger numbers, we get bigger and bigger results. As we start being more and more godly, and more and more content, God knows He can trust us, and then our little world must multiply to go where He needs us to go. Maybe the formula should be:

Godliness + Contentment = Great Gains^2

Thank you for allowing me this time to speak into your life. Keep pressing forward. Your progress will continue to amaze you!

Until we meet again,

HELLWIG

Notes

Day 11

[1] Foster, Richard J. *Celebration of Discipline, the Path to Spiritual Growth.* Harper One; Anniversary edition (February 13, 2018)

Day 16

[2] There are several podcasts I enjoy listening to. I'm sure you have several of your own! The point is, keep the positive words present in your mind to keep you encouraged and moving forward.

Day 22

[3] https://www.americanexpress.com/en-us/business/trends-and-insights/articles/whats-the-future-of-business/

Day 27

[4] https://www.cnet.com/tech/gaming/internet-or-sex-which-would-you-choose/ assessed 03/03/2023

Day 33

[5] Scrivner, Joel. *WINology: 9 Steps to Winning in Life, Business & Relationships.* Blaze Publishing House, 2016

EPILOGUE

[6] Cleveland, Mike

About the Author

JILL HELLWIG

Her Heart

Every once in a while, you meet someone who changes your perspective, someone who challenges you to think bigger, reach higher and bravely embrace change. Jill Hellwig is one of those people.

Jill is the gifted author of *Grow With Goals, A How-To Guide for Activating Your Purpose,* co-author of *When Women Reign*, and she is a Ziglar Legacy Certified inspirational speaker and vision-driven coach. Her unique ability to see the good in every person allows her to mentor, motivate and activate others to fulfill their potential. She is passionate about helping others discover and live from their strengths so they can position themselves for success.

Her Experience

Jill draws from over 25 years of corporate, non-profit and community experience, including three years as a national top 10 territory sales representative with MCI, a $12 billion company, and fourteen years with Ziglar, Inc.

Zig Ziglar fondly referred to her as "The Bear Hunter" for her prowess of producing multi-millions in revenue. Often exceeding quotas by more than 300%, Jill's focus was contributing to the success of her clients whose industries included high-tech, professional services, manufacturing, global firms, and government agencies.

In 2009 Jill left corporate America to serve with her husband in full-time ministry. Upon the birth of their fourth child and first daughter, she became a full-time stay-at-home mom. In the midst of this transition, she began her coaching, consulting and speaking firm, Brand New U Coaching, which is focused on empowering individuals and companies in their professional and personal journeys. Jill also serves alongside her husband at Create Church in Richardson, Texas.

Because of this multifaceted background and her unique ability to touch each person individually right where they are today, you will leave feeling inspired, equipped, and ready to make a difference!

Jill is available for speaking engagements, workshops, or lectures.

Contact Jill at:
jill@brandnewu.org
www.brandnewu.org